Burlesque

Jose Escobar

TITLE SEQUENCE OVER MUSIC
A series of tight CLOSE-UP shots of dancers moving in high energy fast paced sexy choreography. Very provocative. Legs.
Arms. Butts. Boas. Sequins. Costumes. High heels. A kaleidoscope of images and colors.

END TITLES ON A BLACK SCREEN
FADE IN sounds of PEOPLE TALKING -- GLASSES CLINKING -- all the BACKGROUND SOUNDS of a BUSY, HIP NIGHTCLUB. SUDDENLY... a loud DRUM ROLL.
CAMERA is low, moving through BACKSTAGE, passing CURTAINS and the WINGS, flying out onto a shiny black STAGE awash in light. PUSH IN on FOOTLIGHTS which are now blinding us, blasting into camera as they form the word...

BURLESQUE
DRUM ROLL ends with a CYMBAL CRASH. The SCREEN goes BLACK.
Then we hear an opening MUSIC "INTRO", a bawdy QUARTET.
EXTREME CLOSE UP: RED LUSCIOUS LIPS... speaking directly into CAMERA in a smoky, sultry voice.

TESS
Once upon a time ... a long, looong time ago... there was a good little girl... and they called her...
REVEAL ... TESS. A stunner with impossibly long lashes, theatrical make-up and a sequined, skin-tight band-aid of a dress. She works the tight stage of the club, toying with the AUDIENCE.

TESS (CONT'D)
Burlesque.
MUSIC BLARES from a HOT YOUNG BUMPER BAND -- sax, drums, bass -- wearing bowler hats, suspenders and lots of ink. The crowd HOOTS. Lame streamers EXPLODE from the stage.

TESS (CONT'D)
Some say she up and died-of neglect. Abandonment.

(WHISPER)
. old age.
The club's red booths are about half-full with a hip crowd.
Walls cluttered with photos. Celebrities tucked in shadows.

TESS (CONT'D)
But I say... no matter how hard you try, you can't keep a good girl down. And I've got a bevy of 'em.

INT. BACKSTAGE DRESSING ROOM - CONTINUOUS
A DOZEN gorgeous, leggy GIRLS fight for the mirror. Miles of skin. Heavy make-up. Lashes. Boobs. Butts. Fishnets.
Boas. And SEQUINS. Oceans of them. It's definitely decadent. Completely cabaret.

TESS (O. S.)
Come to think of it, none of them are all that good, which isn't all that bad...
SEAN (31), a cute gay guy with an armful of accessories pushes his way through the girls and in a blur, tightens a corset, tosses a boa, adjusts a garter just so.

TESS (O. S.) (CONT'D)
Eight shows a week. Sixteen gorgeous girls. Thirty-two towers of luscious legs...

BACK ON TESS --
Behind her, our GIRLS slink onto the stage one by one.

TESS (CONT'D)
Say hello to Scarlett. Jesse.
Anna. Coco-puff. And Georgie-Girl.
The girls gather at the edge of the stage, lit by footlights, moving in place to the beat of the INTRO MUSIC. Hips sway.
Fingers snap. Tess weaves playfully between them.

TESS (CONT'D)
All of them the creme-de la creme.

(CYMBAL CRASH)
De la creme.
The girls strike nasty, (but funny) provocative poses, etc...

TESS (CONT'D)
Each one a bastion of bodacious...
(Coco bends over, peers between her legs)
Elegance.
TWO GIRLS upside down on chairs NAIL aerial splits.

TESS (CONT'D)
Not to mention their other...
(smacks Coco on the ass)
Ass-ets.
Coco raises a brow, moves her butt to a LOUD BUMP-AND-GRIND.

TESS (CONT'D)
Welcome to the Burlesque Lounge, dead smack in the center of the Sunset Strip-- did I say "strip?"
(cat calls from audience)
I meant TEASE...
FOOTLIGHTS FLARE, UPLIGHTING THE GIRLS. They shift their weight, hitting the beats with risque moves and hip-thrusts as they MOVE DOWNSTAGE suggestively toward the audience to the MUSIC...

EXT. MAIN STREET, GRUNDY, IOWA - NIGHT
A small, grime-streaked steel town, hanging on by the skin of its teeth. Boarded-up storefronts, a run-down A&P. CAMERA
MOVES past an old sign: WELCOME TO GRUNDY!!! and lands on a broken neon sign that reads "DWIG 'S BAR" It flickers so you can read the name: DWIGHT'S. Then goes back to DWIG.

INT. DWIGHT'S BAR - SAME
Chipped paint. Old beer posters. A few pathetic customers.
Beer on tap. Pinball standing lonely in the corner.
A REGULAR drains his beer, tosses down a quarter and starts to leave. Someone stops short at the table.

ALI
Uh, excuse me? You forgot something.
He turns. Sees:
ALI ROSE. One hand holding a bar rag, the other planted on her hip. Ali has a look that's all her own: short shorts, white platform sandals, hair piled up high, more make-up than the rest of Grundy's women combined. She's young -- 22 -- but has a confidence that's got nothing to do with age.

REGULAR
No, that's your tip.

ALI
Huh. See, now that's interesting -- you and I must do math completely differently, cause me? I start with the six beers I brought you, add the four spills I cleaned up, the five times I refilled your peanuts, plus the three times you "accidentally" touched my ass, then
I tack on lying to your wife when she called looking for you, twice, and I come up with a sum that's a hell of a lot more than twenty-five cents.
Before the Regular can respond, Ali is joined by LORETTA --
30's wearing every one of those years hard.

LORETTA

She's just teasing, Ike. You go on home now, and tell Kay I said hi.
The Regular leaves. Loretta picks up the quarter.

LORETTA (CONT'D)
It's better than nothing.

ALI
Nothin's cheap. A quarter's an insult.

LORETTA
It'll cover half a load down at the
Spanky Clean.

ALI
There's only one thing a quarter is good for.
Ali takes the quarter and heads to the back of the room, passing a GEEZER who's sitting by himself, drinking alone.

LORETTA
Oh no, hon, now you know how Dwight feels about that.

ALI
Dwight isn't here.
Ali stops in front of the rinky-dink karaoke machine.

LORETTA
He could come back any minute.

ALI
Tough. I'm not working here for the tips Loretta.
She pops the quarter into the machine and chooses a song.
She picks up the microphone and, after a few opening beats, starts singing ETTA JAMES'S "SOMETHING'S GOT A HOLD ON ME".

ALI (CONT'D)
OOOOOOOOOH, SOMETIMES I GET A GOOD
FEELING, Y-E-A-H
And now we see where the confidence comes from. She's got a voice that's way too big for this town-- the kind that reaches way down inside you and rattles things loose.
WE HEAR the same song continue as we INTERCUT with:

INT. BURLESQUE LOUNGE - ON STAGE - NIGHT
The Girls undulate at the footlights as they sing the chorus:

BURLESQUE GIRLS
YEEEEEEEEAAAAAAAHHHHHH...
WE INTERCUT:
IN DWIGHT'S BAR, Ali is belting now. Loretta is torn between enjoying listening and watching the door for Dwight.

ALI
I GET A FEELING THAT I NEVER,
NEVER, NEVER HAD BEFORE, NO, NO ...
ON THE BURLESQUE STAGE the Girls belt out a raucous chorus.

BURLESQUE GIRLS
YEEEEEEEEAAAAAAAHHHHHH...
As other ENTERTAINERS appear onstage:

TESS
The insatiable La Puccini Triplets!
Death-defying daredevils Missy and
Kitten DeVille! The Countess of contortion, Eva Destruction! And how about a little love for those bad boys of burlesque, our naughty- bawdy bumber band!
THE TATTOOED BAND blares as the troupe kicks in unison IN DWIGHT'S BAR, Ali sings, with a powerful vocal quality reminiscent of Etta James, Sarah Vaughn, Billy Holiday.

ALI
I JUST WANT TO TELL YOU RIGHT NOW,
THAT, OOOH ...
ON THE BURLESQUE STAGE, the GIRLS and the BAND, loud and bawdy.

BURLESQUE GIRLS
OOOOOOOOOOOHHHHHHH!!
IN DWIGHT'S BAR, Ali, letting loose now. Wailing.

ALI
I BELIEVE, I REALLY DO BELIEVE THAT
SOMETHING'S GOT A HOLD ON ME,
YEAH.
ON THE BURLESQUE STAGE, the BURLESQUE GIRLS move in a line toward the audience, confident, sexy. The BARTENDERS,
WAITRESSES and people working at the club sing along.

ALL

OH ... IT MUST BE LOVE!
BARTENDERS
BA-DA, BA-DA, BA-DA:
IN DWIGHT'S BAR, Ali, letting it rip. The Geezer sips his beer, unmoved.

ALI
I'VE GOT A FEELING, I FEEL SO STRANGE. EVERYTHING ABOUT ME SEEMS TO HAVE CHANGED, STEP BY STEP, I GOT A BRAND NEW WALK, EVEN SOUND SWEETER WHEN I TALK. I SAID, OH.
ON THE BURLESQUE STAGE, The Girls.

BURLESQUE GIRLS
OOOOH.
IN DWIGHT'S BAR, Ali.

ALI
OOOH. HEY BABY, IT MUST BE LOVE!
ON THE BURLESQUE STAGE, The Girls form a line.

BURLESQUE GIRLS
YOU KNOW IT MUST BE LOVE.
IN DWIGHT'S BAR, Ali sings.

ALI
YOU KNOW IT WALK LIKE LOVE. IT TALK LIKE LOVE. IN THE MIDDLE OF THE NIGHT, MAKE ME FEEL ALRIGHT:
IN THE BURLESQUE LOUNGE, The Girls, Tess, the other Entertainers, Busboys, Waitresses, Bartenders and entire company do a BIG FINISH.

ALL
BA-DA, BA-DA, BA-DA, BA-DA!
IN DWIGHT'S BAR, Ali finishes the song. Loretta CLAPS. The Geezer, unimpressed, gets up and leaves.

LORETTA
People around here wouldn't know talent if it bit 'em in the Danglies. Where you gotta go is Des Moines. They got karaoke bars where you can win a hundred bucks a night.

ALI

Loretta-- when I get out of this butt-hole of a town, I sure as shit won't be heading for Des Moines.
She hops up onto the bar, spins around on her butt, one leg up in the air like a Varga girl, then hops down on the other side then gets back to work.

INT. BURLESQUE LOUNGE - BACKSTAGE - NIGHT
The audience is still applauding as the Performers crowd into the backstage area, squeezing past the Puccini Triplets preparing their act.
Tess comes off stage and bumrushes Sean.

TESS
Where the hell is Nikki?

SEAN
Rehab, if there's a God.
The BACKSTAGE DOOR BURSTS OPEN revealing--

NIKKI
I heard that.
Nikki, a stunning, feisty brunette, sashays in--

TESS
Jesus, Nikki, you're later than
Georgia's period! Where were you?

NIKKI
Weave, wax, paws and claws.
She drops her bag, quickly peels her clothes off, holds out her arms as Sean slips her corset onto her--
Tess eyes Nikki's body--

TESS
Hold it right there. Weigh in.
Nikki unwillingly steps on the scale. Tess shakes her head.

TESS (CONT'D)
Put on five pounds or I bump you.
Nikki protests as Sean double-takes at Georgia -- who FLITS
BY with a slightly protruding belly.

EXT. TRAILER PARK - IOWA - NIGHT
Ali winds her way through the trailers, carrying a bag of take-out, with a swing in her step -- moving to music playing in her head. She reaches a double-wide, lets herself in.

ALI
Nanna? Got your pot roast here!

INT. ALI'S TRAILER - NIGHT
TV noise. She comes in, kicks off her heels.

ALI
They were out of steak fries, so I got you some of those...
Then she stops in her tracks. Nanna -- 80's, housecoat, oxygen tank -- is slumped in her chair. The TV remote is on the floor. "ENTERTAINMENT TONIGHT" is blaring.

ALI (CONT'D)
Nanna?

EXT. CEMETERY - IOWA - DAY
Loretta and Ali, at the grave with a MINISTER who looks to be about A CEMETERY WORKER is nearby, picking his teeth with a toothpick.

YOUNG MINISTER
Dear Lord, we gather here today not to mourn, but to celebrate the life of Alison Rose.

ALI
Arlene.

YOUNG MINISTER
What?

ALI
She's Arlene. I'm Alison.

YOUNG MINISTER
Oh, shit.
(then, befuddled)
Can I start over?
Ali rolls her eyes.

LATER,
The Minister and the Cemetery worker walk away, leaving Ali and Loretta alone.

LORETTA
You were real good to her, Ali.

ALI
No, she was good to me.
She rearranges the flowers resting on the plot, fixing it up.

ALI (CONT'D)
And she wasn't even my real Nanna.

LORETTA
What... ?

ALI
Foster care. She took me in for the checks. When I turned eighteen, the money stopped coming. She could've kicked me out, but she didn't.

(BEAT)
(MORE)
ALI (CONT'D)
She had a lot of pain at the end.
Nothing she talked about, but I could tell.

LORETTA
Well, then I guess this is a blessing. Now she's free.
ON ALI, thinking realizing:

ALI
(talking about herself)
Yeah. I guess she is.

INT. ALI'S TRAILER - DAY
Nanna's clothes - mostly flowered housedresses -- are folded in paper bags. Her belongings are stacked up in the corner.
CLOSE ON ALI'S MATTRESS, as she pulls a WAD OF CASH out from under it.

HEAR MUSIC OVER: "HONEY ROCK. "
INT. BURLESQUE LOUNGE - ON STAGE - NIGHT
Nikki leads a GROUP OF GIRLS in a raucous routine to "HONEY ROCK". Very Moulin Rouge.

BURLESQUE GIRLS
HONEY:::
In the wings, Tess watches with Sean.

TESS

Girls look good tonight.

SEAN
Amazing what a pink spotlight can do. Hides more cellulite than a burka.

BURLESQUE GIRLS
GO, HONEY, GO!.. '
INT. ALI'S TRAILER - DAY
MOVE IN ON ALI, as she counts the money. Shit. Not enough.
Then she looks around the trailer and realizes - tough shit.
Stuffs the money in a pocket, then pulls out a suitcase.

INT. BURLESQUE LOUNGE - ON STAGE - NIGHT
The Burlesque Girls tease the crowd.

BURLESQUE GIRLS
GO, HONEY, GO!.. '
INT. ALI'S TRAILER - DAY
THE SUITCASE, as Ali throws in her belongings. When it's full, she grabs a stack of records -- Jazz and Soul -- tries to fit them into the suitcase, but it won't close. She picks one: ETTA JAMES. She sticks it in the suitcase and zips it up.

INT. BURLESQUE LOUNGE - NIGHT
BURLESQUE GIRLS
OH, HONEY!
INT. ALI'S TRAILER - DAY
Ali reaches into a drawer, pulls out a FRAMED PHOTO of A
YOUNG WOMAN, 20's, short dress, heavy make-up, holding hands with a 7-year-old girl. Ali slips it into the suitcase pocket. She takes one last look around the trailer.

BURLESQUE GIRLS (O. S.)
GO, HONEY, GO!.. '
EXT. GRUNDY MAIN STRIP - DAY
CLOSE ON ALI'S WHITE PLATFORMS, strutting down the street.

INT. DWIGHT'S BAR - DAY - MUSIC FADES OUT
Ali enters. DWIGHT is at the bar: 50's, beer gut, humorless.

DWIGHT
You're three days late.

ALI
I had a death in the family.

DWIGHT
And what, people stop drinking cause your grandma died? Get your apron and get to work.

ALI
I'm not here to work. I'm leaving.

LORETTA
You are?

ALI
Yeah.

(TO DWIGHT)
I just came for my back pay.

DWIGHT
Payday's the end of the month.

ALI
But, I won't be here then. And you owe me for three weeks.

DWIGHT
I don't owe anyone anything till the end of the month.
Ali sets down her suitcase and marches over to him.

ALI
You know what, Dwight? Contrary to what you've been told, there's no law in Grundy that says you have to spend every waking minute being a tight-fisted, cheap-ass prick --

LORETTA
(trying to intercede)
Ooh, hon, I'm not sure that particular approach is gonna --

ALI
I've spent three years of my life

HERE--
DWIGHT
--And you'll probably spend another three. You want to quit? Good riddance. I'll replace you before you hit the county line, but I sure ain't gonna pay for the privilege.
He walks out the back door, slamming it behind him.

ANGLE ON: THE CASH REGISTER. Ali opens the drawer, pulls out a wad of cash. Peering out back to make sure Dwight isn't coming in, Ali counts out some money.

LORETTA
What are you doing?

ALI
I'm only taking what he owes me.

(THEN)
How much was that bike you been wanting for little Keith?
Ali STUFFS a few TWENTIES into Loretta's apron-- pockets the rest.

LORETTA
Ali-- where are you gonna go?

ALI
Somewhere I can breathe. Now gimme a hug, I gotta get out of here before he gets back.
Loretta hugs her tight, then looks Ali in the eye, concerned.

LORETTA
You can't just head off into the sunset without a plan.

ALI
(RESOLUTE)
Watch me.
Ali gives her one more hug, then grabs her bag and leaves.

MUSIC BACK UP: "HONEY ROCK"
EXT. DOWNTOWN GRUNDY - DAY - CARRY MUSIC
Ali takes off down the street. She passes TWO OLDER WOMEN waiting for a bus. A beat as they watch her pass. Then:

OLDER WOMAN
She'll be back.
As Ali heads off, we HEAR:

BURLESQUE GIRLS
GO, HONEY, GO!.. '
INT. GREYHOUND BUS STATION - GRUNDY, IOWA - DAY
Ali is at the ticket counter.

ALI

How much to Los Angeles?

TICKET BOOTH GUY
One way or round-trip?

ALI
You're kidding, right?

INT. BURLESQUE LOUNGE - ON STAGE - NIGHT - CARRY MUSIC
Cabaret chairs as they DROP FROM THE CEILING. The girls
CATCH them, SPIN them around, SLAM them down and LAND ON THEM

IN VARIOUS LAYOUTS.
IN THE WINGS, Tess hands Sean her corset as she slips into a slinky dress. He takes her cigarette holder and grips it between his teeth as he zips her in.

SEAN
They're loving you tonight.

TESS
They're loving you.

SEAN
Oh, shucks, I just tell myself I'm writing for a big old drag queen.

TESS
Eat me.
As he heads off with her discarded costume:

SEAN
A big old foul-mouthed drag queen!
Tess looks in a mirror. As she makes the necessary adjustments, VINCE SCALI appears. 35, scruffy-handsome.

VINCE
Good show tonight.
She glances up, sees him. Gets icy. Goes back to primping.

VINCE (CONT'D)
Too bad the club's half-empty.

TESS
Half-full.

VINCE
I got another call from Marcus
Gerber.

TESS
And you told him we weren't selling.

VINCE
He wants to raise his offer. I told him we'd hear him out.
Tess spins around, looking him in the eye for the first time.

TESS
Vince, I don't care what the number is; the only way Marcus Gerber will get this club from me is by prying it out of my cold, dead, heavily- jeweled fingers.
She pivots away and sweeps into the club.

BURLESQUE GIRLS
OH, HONEY!!.
Big finish, the number on stage ends.

INT. GREYHOUND BUS - NIGHT
Ali's on the bus, in a seat by herself. A LITTLE GIRL in front of her is peering over the chair, watching Ali. Ali smiles at her. The Little Girl's mother notices, gets the girl to sit down by tickling her.
Ali unzips the pocket on her suitcase, takes out the FRAMED
PHOTO of the mom and girl, looks at it. Then she looks out the window and watches America fly by as DAY TURNS TO NIGHT.

EXT. CITY FREEWAY - DAY - THE BUS - SPEEDING BY
Over which we HEAR someone channel surfing radio static--

INT. BUS - SAME
Ali sits with her radio headset, searching stations as...

RADIO
7 KIIS FM. Broadcasting from
Hollywood and Vine...
Ali perks up-- looks out the window as the bus rounds a bend and... THE HOLLYWOOD SIGN comes into view. NEW MUSIC UP:

EXT. STREET - HOLLYWOOD BLVD. DAY - CARRY MUSIC

The rush of tourists and traffic. Through a sea of people moving down the crowded sidewalk we FIND ALI as she emerges through the crowd, carrying her bags. Looking around at this exciting city. She SPOTS a SHITTY HOTEL with a sign: "$00 a night. " She looks up at it. Then heads across the street--

INT. ALI'S HOLLYWOOD HOTEL ROOM - DAY
Cramped, dingy carpet, chipped paint. Key in the door. The MIDDLE-EASTERN HOTEL MANAGER -- 40's -- leads Ali in, pointing out the features of the room, speaking fast in an impossibly thick Kurdish accent. Ali nods along, not understanding a word. When he stops:

ALI
Okay!

(THEN)
Well. Good luck with that.
He drops her suitcase on the bed and stands there. Waiting.

ALI (CONT'D)
Oh, hang on.
She digs into her purse. All she has is twenties. She peels one off and holds it out.

ALI (CONT'D)
If I could just get a little --
But before she can finish, he pockets it, nods and leaves, closing the door behind him. To the closed door:

ALI (CONT'D)
-- change.
She pulls open the blinds, they fall off the wall with a CRASH! Ali stares at them. Then she opens the window. The SOUNDS OF HOLLYWOOD pour in.
She digs out her cash, sticks it under the mattress. Then she reconsiders.
She removes the money, takes a Ziploc bag full of make-up from her purse, dumps the make-up onto the bed, seals the money up in the Ziploc, and takes it into:
THE BATHROOM. She lifts the lid of the back toilet tank and slips the Ziploc of cash under it, catching the bag in the lid as she sets it back down, so it won't fall in.
She goes back into the main room to find a CALICO CAT sitting on the window sill. It MEOWS, hops into the room.

ALI (CONT'D)
Hey. I thought this was a single.
The cat curls up next to her. She checks his junk.

ALI (CONT'D)
Typical. First guy I meet is neutered.

(THEN)
You don't happen to know anyone in the music business, do you?

CLOSE ON "BACKSTAGE WEST" MAGAZINE,
Ali sips coffee from a paper cup as she reads TRADES and WANT
ADS spread over the floor. She refills the lid of the cup, which the cat laps up.

ALI (CONT'D)
Singer/Actress... Singer/Songwriter
. Singer/Scuba diver? Perfect.
ON ANOTHER AD: It says: "SINGER/WAITRESS WANTED. " MUSIC UP:

EXT. THEME RESTAURANT - DAY
Ali cruises toward the address, dressed in her Iowa best, full of confidence. She rounds a corner and sees:

A LONG LINE OF 165 GORGEOUS, IMPECCABLY GROOMED GIRLS.
Ali stops in her tracks. Tougher competition than she was expecting. She heads for the back of the line, passing girls doing vocal warm-ups. One girl is belting out a riveting "SOMEWHERE OVER THE RAINBOW". Just as Ali gets in line, the door opens and a SKINNY GUY sticks his head out.

SKINNY GUY
Sorry, ladies, that's all the applications we're taking today.
CLOSE ON: an ad: "DANCERS WANTED. PRETTY GIRLS ONLY. "

INT. ALI'S HOLLYWOOD HOTEL ROOM - MORNING
Ali circles the ad, sips coffee. Looks at the cat.

ALI
I can dance.

INT. SEEDY NIGHTCLUB - AFTERNOON
Ali breezes in-- SEES ... a bunch of stripper poles, seedy drunk guys in the audience. She PIVOTS, and walks right back out. As she leaves, a DRUNK GUY turns to A SEEDY GUY.

DRUNK GUY
She'll be back.

CLOSE ON: A FLYER, BEING SNATCHED OFF A BULLETIN BOARD: "BACKGROUND SINGERS FOR URBAN GROUP. "
INT. WAITING ROOM - DAY
Ali enters, full of energy, as 65 hot LATINA and AFRICAN-
AMERICAN girls in butt-baring, hootchie, hip-hop garb, turn in unison and eye her, in her denim shorts and white platforms. Not her crowd.

CLOSE ON: A PEN CIRCLES: "SINGER/DANCERS WANTED FOR TOUR. "
INT. ALI'S HOLLYWOOD HOTEL ROOM - MORNING
Ali, eyeing the ad, sips a cup of coffee. Looks at the cat.

EXT. EDGE DANCE STUDIO - DAY
Ali, dressed like the girls at the video audition: hootchie, street -- opens the door to find 30 CLASSICAL BUN-TOPPED
BALLERINAS stretching, warming up. A Degas painting. They turn in unison and eye her. Again, not her crowd.

EXT. THE CAPITOL RECORDS BUILDING - HOLLYWOOD - DAY
Gleaming in the California sunshine. Ali stares up at the glittering shrine to recording. Takes in the whole swirling, crazy scene around her.

EXT. SUNSET STRIP - NIGHT
Ali wanders down the sidewalk chugging an iced latte. The
Strip hums with SLICK NIGHT LIFE. Expensive cars pull up to valets. Hipsters swish past velvet ropes. Ali moves through the throngs, alone, anonymous, invisible.
She passes a CONSTRUCTION SITE for a 15-STORY-TALL BUILDING, all lit up, guys working at night. A BUS pulls out, spewing exhaust. As the smoke clears, Ali sees, across the street:
A BEAUTIFUL, STATUESQUE GIRL standing on the landing of a fire escape under a street lamp beside a NONDESCRIPT CLUB.
Ali catches glimpses of her as the Sunset traffic whizzes by: full make-up, spangled burlesque costume, impossibly high heels, awesome. This is Coco. Coco makes the dirty streetlight look like a movie-quality Kleig. Everything about her shimmers.
Intrigued, Ali looks for a break in the traffic and crosses the street. As she nears the club, she hears a MAN'S VOICE:

ALEXIS
Like I said, LOOK BUT DON'T TOUCH!
ALEXIS, drag queen/door whore, also in full costume and make- up, TOSSES a GUY out the front door onto the street, then heads back inside--

Ali smiles to herself. Then turns back to look at COCO who disappears inside a BACK DOOR as... NIKKI walks out. Lights a ciggie. She has on full make-up. Lacquered lips. Lashes like peacock feathers. She sees Ali staring.

NIKKI
Didn't your Mama tell you it's not polite to stare?

ALI
Sorry, you're just -- so DAMN beautiful.

NIKKI
(WARMING)
In that case, screw your Mama, stare away.
Nikki strikes a pose, campy, showing Ali her best side. They both laugh.

AL I
No one would ever guess.

NIKKI
What?

ALI
That you're a dude.
Nikki's face turns to stone. Her eyes widen in horror. Ali sees the mistake she made. She's mortified.

ALI (CONT'D)
Oh, shit.

NIKKI
"Shit's" right, you little half-wit

TWAT--
Nikki is about to unleash when the stage door opens.

SEAN
Bitch! You're on!
Sean grabs her and drags her inside. As he does, a STRAND OF CRYSTAL BEADS comes off her costume, falls to the ground.

ALI
I'm really sor--
The stage door slams shut. Ali picks up the strand of beads.

Holds them up in the light, watching them shimmer.
She goes to the front of club, where a smattering of L. A.
HIPSTERS enter. There's a GLASS DISPLAY CASE full of photos of the acts. Ali looks at the pictures of the Girls in their elaborate costumes and provocative poses.
She's unintentionally made her way to the front door. Black curtains obscure her view inside. She peers in. HEARS cool music emanating. The sounds of a nightclub. Intriguing. She ventures inside...

INT. BURLESQUE LOUNGE - NIGHT
Ali MOVES down a DIMLY LIT HALLWAY. More beautiful photos of women in elaborate costumes, drawings, sketches, paintings clutter the walls. Ali follows the photos down the hallway.
MUFFLED SOUNDS penetrate the darkness: people talking over each other, glasses clinking. 1930's Berlin style music.

ALEXIS
I. D. ?
Alexis sits on a stool, glaring down at her.

ALI
What is this place? A strip club?

ALEXIS
Strip club? Honey, I ought to wash your mouth out with Jaegermeister.
The only pole you'll find in here is Natasha the shot girl.
Ali looks back at the photos.

ALEXIS (CONT'D)
(IMPATIENT)
Babycakes, shit or get off the throne, I got a club to fill here.
Ali digs her ID out, hands it over. Alexis scans it --

ALEXIS (CONT'D)
Twenty bucks.
Ali looks in her wallet. Sees one lone twenty inside. She hands it to Alexis. He nods for her to go ahead. Ali descends a staircase INTO THE CLUB...
. and is BOMBARDED by: colors, chaos, laughter, scandal -- all shimmering, as if someone dunked the place in glitter.
And over it all, an incredible mash-up of old music with a contemporary beat tying it all together.
Ali ENTERS, rounds a pillar, staring out into the room as a
SPOTLIGHT finds the stage where half a dozen OSTRICH FANS

PART REVEALING--
TESS
Smoother than honey and twice as sweet. Each girl lovelier then the next. Gentlemen, hold onto your hats. Ladies, hold on to your gentlemen. We may not have windows... but we DO have the best view on the Sunset Strip!
MUSIC KICKS IN AS LIGHTS FLARE from the back of the stage, where Three Girls stand, backs to the audience, Fosse-style.
Coco, Georgia, and Nikki strut downstage. Behind them, Girls
MOVE AND DANCE on cabaret chairs. Totally raunchy, completely timeless.
The girls hit the beats, turning upside-down on cabaret chairs, arched backs, legs reaching upward, bending over, asses to the audience, bodies writhing in air-tight choreography: thrusting hips, whipping heads, stomping feet.
Ali watches, exhilarated, as the music builds and SWELLS to a full on performance with the entire ensemble--

JACK
Get you a drink?
She turns. A bartender is watching her watch. JACK - 25, punky, dark hair, eyeliner, one arm half-sleeved with tats.

ALI
Only if you're buying.

JACK
(slides her a beer)
Welcome to L. A.

ALI
(DISAPPOINTED)
Is it that obvious?

JACK
You still have that new-car smell.

ALI
Not brand new. But still under warranty.

JACK
Where you from?
She looks back at the stage, mesmerized.

ALI
Iowa.

JACK
Oh, yeah? Kentucky. We're practically related.

ALI
I thought you looked familiar.
He smiles. As Ali sips her free beer, Jack stacks drinks on a tray for a DITSY WAITRESS. He slides the tray to her. She doesn't notice. He barks at her:

JACK
Hey_. Go.
The Waitress picks up the tray -- almost spilling the drinks -
- then heads off. Ali looks around the place-- wowed...

ALI
(TO HERSELF)
Damn...

JACK
They don't build 'em like this in
Iowa, huh?

ALI
Hell no. I wouldn't have left.
She stares up at the stage, marvels at the dancers.

ALI (CONT'D)
So tell me -- who does a girl flirt with to get from here...
(points to the stage) to there?

JACK
Is this you flirting?

ALI
With someone wearing more eyeliner than me?
He laughs. Points across the club to A DOOR leading backstage.

JACK
Ask for Tess. She's your guy. Flirt away.
As she heads off--

JACK (CONT'D)
Hey, Iowa-- use my name.

He hands her a card. She looks at it:

ALI
Thanks, Jack.
She smiles, slips it in her cleavage and heads for the door.

INT. BURLESQUE LOUNGE - BACKSTAGE - CONTINUOUS
Ali enters into a frenzy. Legs, costumes, boobs, heels, eyeliners -- all flying around like a flock of birds.
In the middle of the maelstrom sits Tess, at a mirror, quietly applying lipstick.

ALI
Excuse me. I'm looking for Tess.

TESS
(glued to the mirror)
So am I. And sometimes, when the lights are dim, and I squint my eyes ... I can still see her.
She switches to mascara. Sean, arms heavy with corsets, catches eyes with Ali, nods toward Tess: "that's her. " Ali steps closer to Tess.

ALI
Hi. I'm a friend of Jack's, and I'm-

TESS
New in town.

ALI
Yes, and I'm--

TESS
Looking for a job.

ALI
Yes, and I--

TESS
Want to perform here.

ALI
Yes.
Tess glances at Ali in the mirror. Then goes back to her mascara, unimpressed. Silence.

ALI (CONT'D)
I'm a singer. A good one.

TESS
This is a dance show.

ALI
I can dance.

TESS
(a quick glance)
Really? You a professional?

ALI
I'm a quick study.

TESS
Not on my dime.
Tess stands, a final check in the mirror. Ali sees her chance

SLIPPING AWAY--
ALI
Okay, I get that you're busy so I won't waste any more of your time-- but this place-- I've just never seen anything like it before and I know I belong here. So, how can I be a part of it?

TESS
Twenty bucks at the door can make all your dreams come true.
Tess strides out, not looking back. Ali sees the Girls trading glances, amused. She turns and leaves.

INT. BURLESQUE LOUNGE - NIGHT
The Bumper Band plays as Ali makes her way back toward the bar, dejected. Across the room, the Ditzy Waitress, holding an empty tray, flirts with a table of YOUNG HIPSTER GUYS.
Ali sees ANOTHER TABLE OF CHIC CLUBSTERS trying to get the waitress's attention. The Waitress ignores them.
Ali sees the trays on the end of the bar. She grabs one, goes to the TABLE OF CLUBSTERS, clears their empties, takes their order. She finds Jack at the bar, unloads the empties.

ALI
One Dewar's neat, one shot of

Patron, and get this, tough-guy in the hat? He wants a Cosmo.
Jack looks at her, surprised. Impressed.

ALI (CONT'D)
One night. If I'm not 20 times better than boobs-for-brains over there, you don't have to pay me.

MUSIC UP: WAGON WHEEL WATUSI
ON ALI'S WHITE PLATFORM SANDALS, weaving their way through the tables. WIDEN to see she now wears a Burlesque Lounge Cocktail Waitress get-up. She delivers a heavy tray to a table.
She heads back to the bar with empties, eyes glued to the stage, where Coco and the GIRLS are dancing to "Wagon Wheel
Watusi. " As Ali hits the bar, Coco nails a stunning kick.

ALI
Her leg went behind her head!

JACK
Yeah, Coco's the real deal.

ALI
I want to do that.

JACK
She used to dance with the Joffrey
Ballet. Nikki sang opera. Eva performed with Cirque. Everyone here's a pro.
(slides a tray of drinks)
And you're on!

BACKSTAGE,
Nikki, lined up with the other girls, peers between the curtains, spots Ali serving the drinks to a table.

NIKKI
What's she doing here?!

(POINTS)
I want that bitch out. Now.

SEAN
What'd she do to you?

NIKKI
She thought I was a drag queen!
Stifled giggles from the girls.

SEAN
Can't be the first time THAT'S happened.
Nikki is about to haul off on Sean when the CURTAIN OPENS, and WHOOMP!

she turns, flashing her best stage smile as she joins Coco and the Girls onstage in the sexy, high-energy Fosse-style
"Wagon Wheel Watusi. "
From the floor, Ali serves drinks, takes care of customers, all the while watching the spectacle on stage, mesmerized.

INT. ALI'S HOLLYWOOD HOTEL ROOM - NIGHT
The door opens. Ali enters, exhausted, but on Cloud 9, singing "TOUGH LOVER" to herself.

ALI
When he kisses me I get a thrill...
The Cat MEOWS and slinks out from behind the bed. Ali pulls the crystal beads out of her pocket

ALI (CONT'D)
And when he does that wiggle I can't keep still
(ties the beads around the

CAT'S NECK)
Cause he's a tough lover...

INT. BURLESQUE LOUNGE - ON STAGE - NIGHT
"Prince Nez" by Squirell Nut Zippers plays as Eva
Destruction, dressed as a naughty-sexy ballerina, does a bawdy -- and technically flawless -- ballet number on a cabaret chair, on pointe.
ON THE FLOOR, Ali delivers a tray of drinks to a table of
MUSIC-INDUSTRY GUYS. One of them drops a bill on her tray.

ALI
Thanks.
She heads back to the bar. As Jack loads her tray up, she stuffs her tips into her pocket-- SEES Sean, looking her up and down.

SEAN

Okay, girl, time for Sean to give you a real tip.
He ties her shirt up higher, undoes the top few buttons...

SEAN (CONT'D)
You got lips that could suck the chrome off a Peterbilt, but that matte is about as sexy as a bedpan.
As Sean wipes off Ali's lipstick, then whips out a tube of lip gloss and paints away, Jack and Ali share a smirk. Sean steps back, assesses his work. Pleased.

SEAN (CONT'D)
Now baby, go show 'em what you got.
He heads off. While Eva performs onstage, Ali delivers the drinks to a table of SCENESTERS as Eva winds up her act in a flurry of fierce ballet moves, finishing to APPLAUSE as...
Ali notices someone waving her over. MARCUS GERBER. 31, boyishly handsome in jeans and a ringer tee. Gold Rolex, status sneakers. Charming. Charismatic.
When Ali gets to him:

MARCUS
Dewar's on the rocks for me.
Bottle of Dom for the table and--
(tosses a black AmEx on her tray, noticing her)
--And tell Nikki I'm here.
Ali starts away, then--

ALI
And you are?

MARCUS
(nods toward the card)
A member since 1
Oh-kay. He smiles, wickedly handsome. Ali pivots and heads back to the bar. Before she can tell Jack the order:

JACK
Dewar's rocks, bottle of Dom, keep it coming.

ALI
So Asshole's a regular?

JACK
Marcus Gerber. Real estate guy.

ALI
He's with Nikki?

JACK
This week.
Vince goes over to Marcus's table, shakes hands, joins him.

ALI
Who's that with him?

JACK
Technically your boss: Vince Scali.
Tess's partner. And ex...
Jack is about to lift the AmEx off the tray, when Sean swoops by and intercepts it.

SEAN
A black AmEx! The backstage pass to life!
He sees Coco walking by, swipes the AmEx in her cleavage.
She shudders, then turns around and tips her ass up at him.
He swipes the card again.

COCO
Access denied!

SEAN
Now there's a first!
Jack sees Ali laughing at their banter. She heads off with the tray of Dewar's and Dom as the "Prince Nez" number ends.

ON STAGE
LIGHTS UP on TESS, CENTER STAGE as she begins a new number,
"Long John Blues. " A singing/spoken hilarious interlude. The
Girls back her up.

TESS
I GOT A DENTIST, HE'S OVER SEVEN FEET TALL.
HIS NAME IS DR. LONG JOHN,
AND HE ANSWERS EVERY CALL.
I WENT TO LONG JOHN'S OFFICE,
I SAID, "DOCTOR, THE PAIN IS KILLIN' ME. "
HE SAID, DON'T WORRY BABY,
IT'S JUST YOUR CAVITY, NEEDS A LITTLE FILLIN'...
As she continues...

ON THE FLOOR, Nikki is sitting in Marcus's lap, nibbling his neck. Vince sits down beside Marcus. Marcus pats Nikki on the butt, excusing her. As she heads off:

VINCE
She's on the verge.

MARCUS
That's what you said last time.

VINCE
She has no choice. We owe a balloon payment of 100 grand on the first, she took out a second to buy me out of the condo. And she just got turned down for another loan today.

MARCUS
There's a handful of these clubs around town, I could buy one of them tomorrow.

VINCE
But it wouldn't be in the heart of the Sunset Strip.

ON STAGE TESS AND THE GIRLS TOYING WITH THE AUDIENCE...
TESS
. HE TOOK OUT HIS TRUSTY DRILL,
TOLD ME TO OPEN WIDE.
HE SAID HE WOULDN'T HURT ME,
THEN HE FILLED MY HOLE INSIDE.
LONG JOHN, DON ' T YOU EVER GO AWAY.
CAUSE YOU THRILL ME WHEN YOU DRILL ME,
AND I DON'T NEED NO NOVOCAINE TODAY.
HE SAID IF IT EVER STARTS A'THROBBIN',
COME BACK AND SEE OL' LONG JOHN,
AGAIN, AND AGAIN, AND AGAIN AND AGAIN:1:
A RIM-SHOT and BLAST from the band as the audience laughs.
From the stage, Tess notices Vince shake Marcus's hand and leave. A flicker of irritation-- nothing anyone in the audience would notice -- but it's there.

AT THE BAR,
Ali brings a tray of empties over. Sean is there.

ALI
She's funny.

SEAN
Thanks. My lines. Our secret.

Jack gives Sean his drink. He walks off. MUSIC UP: An insanely cool version of Sly and Family Stone "Everybody Is A
Star" mashed up with a Fosse-esque Burlesque rap.
Jack notices Ali watching the stage... she lights up and melts, enraptured by the girls as they vamp to choreography in a tight group.

BURLESQUE GIRLS
(WHISPER RAP A'LA FOSSE)...
Song CONTINUES over a SERIES OF SHOTS:
IN ALI'S HOTEL ROOM, Ali plops down a bunch of BOOKS, OPENS
The Golden Age of Burlesque", lays on her bed, petting her cat with her foot. She locks in on a photo of 20's-era
Burlesque dancers over which we HEAR--

SLY AND FAMILY STONE
EVERYBODY IS A STAR ...
IN THE CLUB, BURLESQUE GIRLS strike a similar pose

BURLESQUE GIRLS
(WHISPER RAP A'LA FOSSE)
ALI CHANNELING THE CHOREOGRAPHY AS SHE:
- wipes down tables with Jack in the club after hours,
- flips through old Soul records at a used LP store,
- pokes her way through the scruffy street folks that hang out by her hotel.

IN THE CLUB
BURLESQUE GIRLS (CONT'D)
(WHISPER RAP A'LA FOSSE)
ON ALI'S BED, Ali flips to a picture of Mae West
IN THE CLUB, Tess cracks up the crowd

BURLESQUE GIRLS (CONT'D)
(WHISPER RAP A'LA FOSSE)
IN ALI'S HOTEL ROOM, Ali eats Chinese take-out as she pores over the book. Turns the page to a photo of OLD SCHOOL
ACROBATS over "Everybody Is A Star"...
IN THE CLUB, Daredevils Missy and Kitten DeVille nail an

AERIAL MOVE
BURLESQUE GIRLS (CONT'D)
(WHISPER RAP A'LA FOSSE)
IN ALI'S HOTEL ROOM, Ali, in the bath, still reading, turns the page to a gorgeous image of Josephine Baker

SLY AND FAMILY STONE
EVERYBODY WANTS TO SHINE. OOH AND
COME OUT ON A CLOUDY DAY ...
IN ALI'S HOTEL ROOM, Ali vamps, dancing to the song in her room in a t-shirt and undies.
The cat watches her, yawns and slinks away.
IN THE CLUB, The Burlesque Girls thwack down on chairs.

BURLESQUE GIRLS
(WHISPER RAP A'LA FOSSE)
IN ALI'S HOTEL ROOM, Ali thwacks down on an old mustard- colored chair.

SLY AND THE FAMILY STONE
EVER CATCH A FALLIN STAR. AIN'T NO
STOPPING TIL IT'S IN THE GROUND...
IN THE CLUB, AN OVERHEAD SHOT, THE BURLESQUE GIRLS now in different costumes in a BUSBY BERKELEY cluster, AS CAMERA
BOOMS DOWN ON THEM and they separate to reveal:
ALI, center stage, belting UP AT CAMERA:

ALI
EVERYBODY IS A STAR::::
SLAM CUT TO --
FIND Ali, in her waitress outfit, watching the girls on stage, lost in her fantasy. She catches herself, then moves along serving drinks while the Girls work the stage.
The Burlesque Girls continue their Burlesque Rap. When the girls thrust out their hips in unison, Ali does too, unconsciously dancing along with them.
AT THE BAR, Jack notices. Watches. Tries to focus on pouring drinks, but his eyes keep drifting to Ali's hips.
NEARBY, Sean notices Jack noticing. Looks from Jack to Ali.
Eyebrow goes up. Interesting.

INT. BURLESQUE LOUNGE - BACKSTAGE - NIGHT
Backstage mayhem. Girls scurry, Sean fusses, Tess sits at the mirror, applying a fake eyelash as WE HEAR a surprisingly good woman's voice BELTING a SONG! It's Nikki. Late again.

TESS
Nikki, do you even own a watch? Or do you measure time in Patron shots?
Ali enters with a tray of drinks. Nikki swipes one.

ALI

Hey, no, that's for --
Nikki opens a bottle, pops 3 pills in her mouth, washes them down with the drink, and sets the empty glass on Ali's tray.

ALI (CONT'D)
You, I guess.
Nikki turns to the mirror and starts getting to work. As Ali hands out the other drinks:

ALI (CONT'D)
Tess? Do you have a second?
Tess doesn't answer. But a slight glance at Ali in the mirror shows she's half-listening.

ALI (CONT'D)
I was thinking -- see, I grew up listening to all this music, I'd play the records over and over --

TESS
Fast-forward, babe. I gotta rebuild
Rome in the next two minutes--

(CALLING OUT)
--SOMEONE TALK TO DAVE ABOUT THE
VOCALS ON THE NEW TRACKS!!!
ALI
Now see-- that's what I've been thinking about. There's one thing I don't get.

TESS
Just one?

ALI
It's the vocals. You have the girls lip-synching. which is fine,
I guess, but wouldn't it be so much better if they actually sang?
The Girls trade looks, knowing Ali's overstepping here. Ali doesn't feel the vibe-shift, surges ahead.

ALI (CONT'D)
I've been reading up on it, and back when burlesque started, that's what they did.
Silence. Nobody moves. All eyes on Tess.

SEAN
Oh, no she didn't?
Tess slowly spins around in her chair to face Ali. Peers at her with a supercilious gaze.

TESS
"When burlesque started"? Which was... when?

ALI
(searching her memory)
Oh. Well... this book said it came after...

TESS
Vaudeville -- is the word you're looking for. Derived from the 15th- century French expression "voix de ville" -- "voice of the city".
Popular songs of the time that were strung together into stage shows.
Which, over time, gave birth to another kind of show in which talented girls showing a bit more skin danced, did skits, and, _ yes, sang. In addition to being raunchier, these shows were funnier, hence the new name.
"Burlesque": "comical" in French.
Ali sees the Girls enjoying this dressing-down immensely.
Tess stands, peers down her nose at Ali.

TESS (CONT'D)
Dance major. Juilliard. I did my thesis on Burlesque.

ALI
Oh. Ok. It's just-- It's just that ... I CAN sing and--

TESS
We can all sing. But they don't come to hear us sing. They come to see the best dancers in town backed by the greatest singers in history.
(then, condescending)
But tell you what: when you find someone with better pipes than
Sarah Vaughn, Billie Holiday and
Etta James-- you let me know.
She sashays out leaving Ali standing there with what's left of her dignity and an empty cocktail tray. The Girls launch back into prepping for the show.

INT. BURLESQUE LOUNGE - BATHROOM - NIGHT
Ali pushes in, pissed off, and hears the sound of PUKING.
She sees Georgia's BOOTS sticking out from under the stall.

ALI
Georgia? You okay in there?
A FLUSH. The stall door opens. Georgia comes out shakily with mascara-smudged eyes, sweet as ever.

GEORGIA
I don't know why they call it morning sickness when it hits at every freakin hour of the day.
She rinses her mouth out at the sink.

ALI
There aren't many women who could dance the Charleston on a chair at -
- what are you, three months?
Georgia turns sideways to the mirror, inspecting her bump.

GEORGIA
Four. Can you believe my boyfriend hasn't noticed yet?

ALI
You haven't told him?

GEORGIA
I guess as long as he doesn't know,
I can still imagine he'll be happy about it.
(looks in the mirror)
Oh my God, look what the cat dragged in.
She gets to work wiping away her smudged mascara.

ALI
You look pretty hot to me.
Georgia reaches into her corset, yanks one breast skyward, then does the same to the other.

GEORGIA
Yeah, well -- you take what Mother
Nature gave you and milk the hell out of it, right?
Coco enters carrying a glass of tonic for Georgia.

GEORGIA (CONT'D)
Thanks, Coco.

COCO
(TO ALI)
Shouldn't you be on the floor?

ALI
I had to pee. Is that okay with you?

COCO
Not when you're blocking my mirror it's not.
Ali sees she's in the way. As she steps aside:

COCO (CONT'D)
(re. the music)
That's us. You okay, or are you gonna puke on me during the number?

GEORGIA
I can't make any promises.
Coco drags her out, leaving Ali alone. Ali looks at herself in the mirror. Reaches into her shirt and does the boob-hoist that Georgia did. Looks again. Better.

INT. ALI'S HOLLYWOOD HOTEL BUILDING - HALLWAY - NIGHT
Ali trudges up the stairs, tired. Suddenly, TWO YOUNG THUGS barrel down the stairs, past her, almost knocking her over.

ALI
Hey!
They tear past her. She shakes her head, reaches her landing, heads down the hall toward her room, then sees:
HER HOTEL ROOM DOOR, ajar. The lock broken.

ALI (CONT'D)
No. No!
She runs down the hall.

INT. ALI'S HOLLYWOOD HOTEL ROOM - NIGHT
Ransacked. Ali rushes in, goes straight into:

INT. ALI'S HOLLYWOOD ROOM - BATHROOM - NIGHT
The lid is off the toilet tank. Her Ziploc of money is gone.

ALI
No!!! God damn it!!!
She looks out the window, SEES the ROBBERS running off, disappearing down the street. She kicks the trash can. It flies across the room.

ALI (CONT'D)
Damn it! Damn it, damn it, damn it, damn it, damn it!
She sees the cat watching her from behind the bed.

ALI (CONT'D)

A lotta help you were.
The cat creeps out, slinks around her legs. Ali plunks on the bed.

ALI (CONT'D)
Shit.
Then she sees, on the floor, the PHOTO she took from Nanna's.
She picks it up. The glass has cracked, tearing the picture.
She takes the picture out of the broken frame, smooths it out
-- then looks around her trashed room. Fighting despair.

EXT. WEST HOLLYWOOD STREET - NIGHT
FOLLOW a motorcycle up the street. The DRIVER has a KEYBOARD on his back. He parks, gets off, takes off his helmet. It's
Jack. He heads for his apartment, but slows when he sees:
ALI, sitting on his steps, her bags at her feet. Head low.

JACK
Ali? What's wrong? You okay?
She tries to speak, but can't -- so she just nods.

JACK (CONT'D)
Really? Cause, in my experience-- when you're on someone's doorstep surrounded by everything you own, there's usually a not-so-good story

THAT--
ALI
I-- WAS--
And as she expected, as soon as she talks, she starts to cry.

ALI (CONT'D)
--RO-0-0-0-OBBED.
JACK
Shit. No way!

ALI
(halting, gaspy sobs)
Came in -- busted the lock-- and stole all my MO-NEY-EY-EY-EY!!!
She sobs--trying to talk, with high-pitched SQUEAKS only heard by birds. Jack winces, trying to follow--

ALI (CONT'D)
(more gaspy sobs)
And there's no way I-- sleep there-- with-- like that-- the manager said-

- not till Monday-- and I don't-- anyone else-- but then-- so I remembered I had... but it went straight to... so I...
She reaches in her pocket, pulls out a card. It's Jack's that he gave her in the club. It has his address on it.

JACK
Okay. I have no idea what you just said, but come on in here and we'll get it sorted out.
She looks at him. Wiping her tears. He picks up the heaviest of her bags and leads her to:

INT. JACK'S APARTMENT - NIGHT
Tiny one-bedroom. Very "done. " Floral sofa. Curtains that match the area rug. Candle groupings.

JACK
Have a seat. I'll get us BOTH a drink. Here --
He hands her his phone. She looks at it.

JACK (CONT'D)
-- call whoever you want, long- distance, whatever--

ALI
I can't.

JACK
Sure you can. Go ahead.
Her chin starts quivering all over again.

ALI
I... don't ... have anyone.

JACK
What do you mean?

ALI
To call.

JACK
No parents?
(she shakes her head)
Siblings? Aunts? Uncles?

(NO AGAIN)
Friends?

ALI
(THROUGH TEARS)
No one! No one, okay? Do I have to spell it out for you? I am -- completely -- alone!
Jack susses out the situation.

JACK
(REALIZING)
So... you're not here to use my phone.
She starts to cry again.

JACK (CONT'D)
Okay. Wait. No, stop, stop, stop, it's okay, it's fine. You'll crash here. No problem. Just, please -- no more crying.
She nods. He grabs a bottle of Tequila and a couple of glasses. Pours them a couple. They both take a drink.

JACK (CONT'D)
Better?
She nods.

JACK (CONT'D)
Okay. Good.
She wipes her eyes.

ALI
Just for one night, I swear. Just till it's light outside and I can figure out my next move.

JACK
Deal.
Then she opens her small bag and the cat strolls out.

JACK (CONT'D)
Whoa, whoa, you didn't say anything about a cat.

ALI
What? You don't like cats?
It slinks around his leg. He shakes it off.

JACK
I hate cats.

ALI

How can you hate a cat?

JACK
It's easy, I'll show you.
The cat bolts into the bedroom.

JACK (CONT'D)
Where's it going? If that thing pees on my bed --

ALI
He goes outside. We just have to open a window. He's very independent.
She opens the window. The cat scurries back in, leaps onto the ledge. Ali pets him. Looks at Jack, smiles.

ALI (CONT'D)
I don't have a name for him yet.
It purrs. Jack eyes it warily.

JACK
One night?

ALI
One night.

INT. JACK'S APARTMENT - LATER
IN THE LIVING ROOM, the lights are low. Ali's on the couch, under covers, cat at her feet. INTERCUT WITH:
THE BEDROOM. Jack at his keyboard, playing from sheet music, learning a song. When he pauses, from the living room:

ALI
You're good.

JACK
Thanks.

ALI
Why don't you play at the club?

JACK
Make more money bartending.

ALI

You in a band?

JACK
Was... Guitarist moved to Reno,
Drummer went to med school, bassist is in rehab. I'm subbing around town till I regroup.
This is for a punk fusion band -- their keyboardist is a flake, so they call me a lot.

ALI
(SARCASTIC)
A flaky punk-rock-fusion keyboardist? No way.
He smiles. Continues playing.
HIGH ANGLE, seeing both of them on either side of a wall.
Her listening, him playing. After a few measures:

ALI (CONT'D)
Hey...
He stops playing again.

ALI (CONT'D)
Why'd you leave Kentucky?

JACK
Why'd you leave Iowa?

ALI
Cause I looked around and realized there wasn't one person whose life
I wanted.

JACK
Exactly.
A beat. Then as he starts playing again:

ALI
Hey Jack?
He stops again.

ALI (CONT'D)
Thank you. I'm really glad I'm not alone tonight.
He smiles.

JACK
Get some sleep.
He continues playing. She closes her eyes.

INT. JACK'S APARTMENT - BEDROOM - MORNING
Light rain on the window.
CLOSE ON: THE CAT'S FACE, staring right into camera.
REVERSE ON: Jack, waking up. As his eyes open, the Cat licks him on the mouth.

JACK
Aauuuuggggghh.
He hurls the cat away and bolts out of bed, disgusted.

INT. JACK'S APARTMENT - LIVING ROOM - NIGHT
Jack straggles in, wiping his mouth. The sofa's made up, blankets folded. Ali is making breakfast, her back to him.
He can't help but notice she's only wearing a tiny tank top and undies. She hears him clear his throat.

ALI
Morning. Coffee?

JACK
(NODS)
Black. Like my soul.
She pours him a cup. Sees a picture of a BEAUTIFUL GIRL on his fridge.

ALI
She's pretty. Your sister?

JACK
My fiancee. Natalie.

ALI
Fiancee? You're straight?

JACK
Of course I'm straight. You thought I was gay?

ALI
Yes?

JACK
Why?

ALI

I don't know, the... make-up?

JACK
It's a look.

ALI
Okay.

JACK
A straight look.

ALI
Okay.

(THEN)
And the floral couch... ?

ALI/JACK
Natalie.
As Ali realizes she's barely dressed in front of a straight guy.

ALI
I should put on pants.

JACK
Probably.
She bolts out to the living room, starts digging through her bag, bent over. She's in the doorway, so from the kitchen, all he can see is her cute little ass sticking out.

ALI
Where is she?

JACK
New York. Doing a play.

ALI
For how long?

JACK
Six more weeks.
She can't find pants. She shifts, so now her ass is facing him directly. He tries not to look--

ALI
(KEEPS DIGGING)
Oh, God, now I feel bad about this.

I'M SORRY--
JACK
For what?

ALI
I don't know. Now that you're straight and engaged, it feels weird that I came here.

JACK
Well, you did, and it was fine.
Aha! Pants. She pulls them out, starts putting them on. He looks out. Her foot is caught in the pants leg. As she hops around, trying to untangle it--

JACK (CONT'D)
Or at least it will be as soon as you get dressed.
She tumbles out of view, thumps against some furniture.
She appears in the doorway, pants on, pulling on a sweater.
She slips her feet into her shoes.

ALI
Alrighty then-- I'll get outta your hair now...

JACK
Wait, where're you headed?

ALI
Oh, don't worry about me. I've got a plan.
(scoops up the cat)
Come on, cat.
She zips the cat into the bag he came in.

JACK
Hang on, let me at least spot you some cash. I'm a little strapped, but I could --

ALI
No, I'm good, if you could just
She nods at the door. He opens it for her.

ALI (CONT'D)
Thank you. For everything. You are my knight in shining... eyeliner.

(MORE)
ALI (CONT'D)
(out the door)
I'll see you at the club.

JACK
Cool.
She leaves. He closes the door behind her. Stands there.

EXT. JACK'S APARTMENT - DAY
Ali looks at the rain. Then marches out into it, lugging her stuff. Goes about 15 yards in one direction, then stops.

INT. JACK'S APARTMENT - SAME
Jack watches her out the window as she marches 15 yards in another direction, then stops. Pondering. She sees a bus stop across the street. She crosses to it and sits.

EXT. BUS STOP - DAY
Ali peers down the street for the bus. Jack appears beside her, getting soaked in the rain.

JACK
So, this plan of yours?

ALI
. was to sit here at the bus stop and come up with a plan.

JACK
Come back inside.

ALI
No, Jack, I--

JACK
ALI--
ALI
I'll figure it out, this is not

YOUR PROBLEM--
JACK
It's pouring!

ALI

It's only water for chrissakes--

JACK
GOD DAMN IT! GET YOUR ASS BACK IN
MY HOUSE! NOW!
ALI
Jack-- you've done enough and--
In ONE MOVE he SCOOPS HER up as she lets out a WHOOOOP!

ALI (CONT'D)
Jack-- No! Stop it!
He grabs her bags and carries her back across the street--

INT. JACK'S APARTMENT - DAY
The DOOR KICKS OPEN-- they ENTER, Jack carrying Ali, dripping wet.

ALI
PLEASE PUT ME DOWN--
He sets her down--

JACK
Look, you have nowhere to go, I have a couch. You may as well stay here for a few days.

ALI
You really don't need to do that.
I'll be fine --

JACK
You'll be homeless. You always have this much trouble saying yes when someone is trying to help you?

AL I
It's never happened before.
The Cat jumps up on the back of a chair, all wet, and SHAKES, splattering them with wet cat smell.

JACK/ALI
Aaaaargh!
As his PHONE RINGS.

JACK
There's a towel in the bathroom-- dry yourself and that damn cat off.
Ali collects the cat-- heads for the bathroom. Jack checks his phone. Answers.

JACK (CONT'D)
(INTO PHONE)
Hey, baby, how's it going?...
Really? That's awesome...

ALI (O. S.)
(CALLING OUT)
DO YOU HAVE A BLOW DRYER?
JACK
(INTO PHONE)
That... ? Just this person from work
What? No, she's just a friend,
I'm helping her out. Nat, it's nothing.
O. S. MUSIC UP: "BABY YOU'VE GOT WHAT IT TAKES" by Brook Denton and Dinah Washington over...

INT. BURLESQUE LOUNGE - ON STAGE - DAY
CLOSE ON A HEAVILY MADE-UP GIRL as she screams and drops out of the shot in a flying split. Behind her, a ROW OF DANCERS do the same. Typical, fantastic, old-school can-can.
WIDEN to see Tess and Sean, on the floor, auditioning them.
The club is brightly lit, none of its evening aura.
Scattered around the club are other HOPEFULS in groups, waiting for their turn.

MUSIC CONTINUES OVER:
EXT. BURLESQUE LOUNGE - DAY
Jack's motorcycle pulls up to the club, with Jack driving, and Ali riding on back.

INT. BURLESQUE LOUNGE - DAY
Ali and Jack enter as the auditions are under way. As they set up the bar, Ali watches the stage, intrigued.
MONTAGE: the dancers auditioning, in small groups. All shapes, sizes. Ali watching. Finally only a few are left.

TESS
Okay, front row, thank you very much.
They walk off stage, dismissed. Tess turns to Sean.

TESS (CONT'D)
What happened to all the great dancers in L. A?

SEAN

They're busy "Dancing with the
Stars. "
(to the waiting dancers)
Last group, please.
HALF A DOZEN DANCERS move to the stage. Ali watches from behind the bar, thinking. Then, on her face, we see: an idea forming.
ON THE FLOOR, Tess and Sean check their clipboards, organizing for this next set. They look up and start in:

TESS
All right, ladies, and five, six, seven -- whoa.
There, in the back row, is Ali, in her white platform shoes.

TESS (CONT'D)
What the hell do you think you're doing?
Coco and Georgia ENTER-- surprised to see Ali on stage.

ALI
Trying out.

TESS
I don't think so.

ALI
Tess, I've been singing and dancing my whole life and--

TESS
The girls here have years of training and experience. This stage is for serious and professional

DANCERS WHO--
ALI
(angry, interrupting)
Hey_. This is your club and you can be as rude as you want--but don't you dare tell me I'm not serious.
Sean's eyebrows reach for the ceiling as Nikki enters, SEES
Ali on stage.

ALI (CONT'D)
I may not have been to a professional dance school, but I have a lot of talent and I came to this town to do something with it.
And the only reason I've been putting up with all the bullshit
"attitude" I get from you is cause

I want to do it here.

(BEAT)
For the first time in my life, I don't want to be someplace else. So you're gonna give me MY shot. Right here. Right now.
Everyone in the club just stands there. Jaws dropped. Tess just looks at her, blinks, incredulous.

ALI (CONT'D)
One song. You don't like it, I'll quit and do us both a favor.

(BEAT)
Your call, lady. I know every number in the show.
Sean, eyes big as saucers, looks from Ali to Tess, then back

AGAIN--
TESS
(DOUBTFUL)
You know every number.

ALI
Which one do you wanna see?
Tess looks at her in disbelief.

ALI (CONT'D)
I said, which one do you wanna see?
Ali just stares at her. Calling her bluff, Tess yells up to
DAVE in the sound booth--

TESS
Tough Lover!
Tess plops down in a booth-- crosses her arms indignantly.
ON STAGE, the music starts. Ali readies herself, starts to dance. Behind a beat to two.
She's got the steps right, but it isn't clicking. She's thinking too hard. No personality.
After a few measures, Tess has seen enough.

TESS (CONT'D)
Okay then, next?

ALI
Hang on.
(to Dave in the booth)
Start it again, please?

As Dave resets the music. Ali regroups: takes her hair down and shakes it loose.
Nikki ENTERS, SEES Ali on stage--

NIKKI
(TO GEORGIA)
What the hell's going on?

COCO
Shhhh.
On stage, Ali takes a beat; inhales, breathing in attitude.
Then she looks up at the booth again.

ALI
Anytime.
The MUSIC starts in again. And this time, Ali comes alive.
She may not have perfect technique or the best extension, but she exudes an ambition and sexuality no one has seen from her before. It's like she becomes a woman before our eyes. She misses a step or two, but who the hell cares?
On the floor, Sean gapes, eyes popping. Tess is poker-faced.
Coco and Georgia's expressions turn from dubious to respectful. Nikki's eyes narrow.
At the bar, Jack freezes, a huge rack of glasses in his arms -
- unable to tear his eyes away.
As the SONG CLIMAXES, Ali finishes with an alluring toss of her ass, then lands in a sexy layout on a chair, owning the stage. The music ends. A stunned silence. The only sound is Ali's heavy breathing.
Then Georgia jumps up, APPLAUDING EFFUSIVELY.

NIKKI
What are so you happy about, that's your replacement.

GEORGIA
Yeah, but she's really good.
Tess and Ali are in a stare down.

TESS
I want so badly to say something bitchy, but nothing's coming.

SEAN
There's a first.
Tess sighs, not wanting to give Ali any props.

TESS
You were off the whole second half.

ALI
So, I was spot on the first half?
Tess narrows her eyes at Ali. Then looks over at Nikki, Coco and Georgia. Georgia gives an effusive THUMBS UP-- then suddenly becomes overcome by nausea, covers her mouth and
RUNS to the bathroom to puke--
Tess rolls her eyes, looks back at Ali.

TESS
Oh, you're gonna be such a pain in my ass.
Ali tries hard not to beam--

ALI
Do I have the job, or not?

TESS
You're not great. What you are is lucky. Because I need someone tonight.

ALI
And I know all the routines.
As Tess turns and leaves--

TESS
Even in those shoes that time forgot.

SEAN
Theeeere's bitchy.
Nikki watches Tess go-- turns and pours herself a shot.

NIKKI
Well-- this totally sucks ass.
Sean jumps up on the stage.

SEAN
Congratulations. The last time someone showed Tess balls like that, she married him.
(looks Ali over)
You look like a checker at a Mal
Wart in Wichita. Just tripled your salary. Get a new look.

ALI
Hey, I happen to like the way I look.

SEAN
Really? That's a fascinating story.
And then what happens?

(ALL BUSINESS)
Backstage in five.

(WALKING OFF)
Welcome to the family.
Ali jumps off the stage, runs to the bar, where Jack is still standing, slack-jawed. She throws her arms around him.

ALI
Sorry for the short notice, I quit!
(plants a big kiss on him)
But hey-- with my raise I'll be off your couch in a week.
She squeezes him tight-- then heads backstage leaving him standing there, really turned on.

INT. BURLESQUE LOUNGE - BACKSTAGE - DAY
Sean swings open A DOOR, revealing a room packed to the gills with costumes: feathers, sequins, fishnets, corsets, jammed up against each other. Sean tosses her clothes in a blur.

SEAN
First number, second number, third number...
She catches the clothes. He dumps shoes on top of them, holding them up as he tells her what they go with:

SEAN (CONT'D)
With the sequined bustier. With the shorts and garters. With the beaded number. And those --
(points to hers)
I never want to see again.

(REMEMBERING)
Oh! And --
He hands her a prop GOLD MACHINE GUN.

SEAN (CONT'D)
For "Miss Otis Regrets". Just be sure you don't --
Ali pulls the trigger. BOOM -- GLITTER SPLATS all over Sean.

SEAN (CONT'D)

Pull the trigger.

MUSIC UP: "RICH MAN'S FRUG". CARRY MUSIC OVER:
INT. BURLESQUE LOUNGE - ON STAGE - NIGHT

The chic audience watches the Girls doing a swingin' sixties shimmy and shake number. CAMERA MOVES ACROSS the girls' faces as drums roll and their heads turn to each drumbeat.

The last face to turn is ALI'S. In FULL STAGE MAKE-UP, she looks like a gorgeous classic burlesque dancer. The girls, in 20's revealing bathing suits and stilettos, kick and dance downstage in a line. Ali struggles a little to keep up

A WAITER CROSSES FRAME and we WIPE TO:

- ANOTHER NIGHT. SAME MUSIC, different costumes. Ali's dancing is improving. WAITRESS CROSSES FRAME and we WIPE TO:

- ANOTHER NIGHT. SAME MUSIC, yet another set of costumes.

Ali's as good as anyone else up there. AN AUDIENCE MEMBER crosses frame and we WIPE TO:

- ANOTHER NIGHT. SAME MUSIC, another set of costumes. Ali knows the steps now, she's not thinking about them. She's all performance, vamping to the audience, selling like crazy.

She NAILS a final layout on a chair, it's flawless.

Tess and Sean are watching from the wings. They notice the extra whip in Ali's head, the bump in her grind.

SEAN

Admit it. You like her. It kills you, but you like her.

Tess meets his eye, then walks away. The number ends. The girls rush offstage and peel their costumes off.

ALI

My tits are up around my ears, my thong's about a mile up up ass, this corset is so tight, I haven't breathed since Tuesday and these lashes are thick enough to kick up a stiff wind.

SEAN

It's fun being a girl, huh?

ALI
(BIG SMILE)

Yeah.

She hands him the last bits of her costume.

FOLLOW Ali as she heads to the dressing room. As she grabs her T-shirt and jeans:

JESSE

I'm starving, who wants to go grab some pizza before the next show?

A general chorus of "Yeah?" and "I'm in. "
FOLLOW Ali to the bathroom as she throws on her clothes and washes off her make-up, humming "Rich Man's Frug" to herself.
She heads back out to the dressing room to find:
EVERYONE IS GONE. She looks around. Feels like an fool.
She plunks down in a chair. Drops her bag on the floor.
Looks at herself in the mirror.
She sees a picture of A CLASSIC BURLESQUE BEAUTY taped to the mirror. Notices her eye make-up -- strong, thick eyeliner.
Ali picks up a brush, dips it in eyeliner, and tries to duplicate the look on her own eye. After a first try:

TESS (O. S.)
Your brush is for shit.
She turns and sees Tess in the doorway. Tess comes over, takes Ali's brush. Looks at it.

TESS (CONT'D)
Where'd you get this, the 99 cent store?
She chucks it in the trash.

ALI
Hey.

TESS
Make-up is like wine. The good stuff costs a fortune but is worth every penny. Where is everyone?

ALI
All the girls went out for pizza.

TESS
Aren't you one of the girls?

ALI
Apparently not.
Tess reads her like a book. Knows what went down. She turns to leave, then pauses at the door. Turns back.

TESS
Don't take it personally. Their love's the kind you gotta earn.
Ali meets her eyes in the mirror. Then Tess grabs a brush from her own station, tosses it to Ali.

TESS (CONT'D)
Dip it in water first, or you'll never get a clean line.
She leaves Ali alone.

INT. JACK'S APARTMENT - BATHROOM - DAY
Jack enters in boxers, kicks them off, opens the shower, then freezes.

JACK
ALI!!!
INT. JACK'S APARTMENT - LIVING ROOM - DAY
Ali is just waking up.

JACK
Your stupid cat peed in the tub!

ALI
What... ?
(sees the window closed)
You closed the window, what do you expect?

JACK
Your cat pees in the house, and it's my_ fault?!
Ali scoops the cat up.

ALI
Awwww. Poor guy, you must have been desperate.

JACK
Goddamn cat. And you used my towel again.
(then, pointed)
How's that apartment hunting coming?
He GRABS the newspaper and tosses it in front of her-- she glares at him, then glances at the paper--

ALI
(EYES WIDENING)
A thousand bucks for a studio?

JACK
Can you really put a price on privacy? Freedom? Your own bathroom? With clean towels?

ALI

Okay, Jack-- I get it--
His cell phone rings. As he checks who's calling:

JACK
Natalie.
(then, into phone:)
Hey, baby, how are you?
He heads into the bedroom, closes the door. Ali shakes her head, begins to peruse the classifieds.

INT. JACK'S APARTMENT - KITCHEN - DAY
Ali, in pajamas, is at the table, combing the classified apartment ads. The cat is beside her.

ALI
Guest studio, Hollywood, $900, with a yard, and -- oh. No pets.
(to the cat)
Screw them.
She scans the ads some more. Finds a good one.

ALI (CONT'D)
Ooh?
Jack walks in. Looks like he's got something on his mind.

ALI (CONT'D)
I think I found my new place.
Where's Pomona?

JACK
Go to Hell, turn left, it's three miles down on the right.

ALI
Really. How's Beachwood Canyon?

JACK
Great, if you have a car.

(BEAT)
Truth is, you should get a car first. This is L. A. You don't exist without a car. Plus, you can't really afford a decent place yet.

(THINKING)
Tell you what.

(MORE)
59
JACK (CONT'D)
I'm gonna suck it up and let you stay here a little longer. Just throw in a little something for rent.
She looks at him, curious.

ALI
What about the "God damn" cat?

JACK
Hey, I don't like the cat. And I don't like my towel being wet. I don't like the lack of privacy. But you're in a jam -- and I'm the kind of guy, if a friend's in trouble, I help. It's just who I am.

ALI
(SUSPICIOUS)
What did Natalie have to say?

JACK
Nothing, you know just... hi.
She narrows her eyes at him. He concedes.

JACK (CONT'D)
And... her play got extended three more months, so since she has to pay rent there, she can't also keep up her part of the rent here.

ALI
Ah-hah.

JACK
So if you could stick around and chip in, it would --

ALI
Save your ass?

JACK
-- help.
Ali looks down at his shoes.

ALI
Well, will you look at that? The shoe, on the other foot!

JACK
OKAY --
ALI
One minute I'm a freeloader with a
God damn cat, the next, I'm the only thing standing between you and

EVICTION --
JACK
Just -- yes or no?

ALI
What's the proposal, exactly?
Jack looks at her-- realizes he's screwed.

JACK
The bedroom, with private bathroom access, for 600 a month, including utilities.

ALI
Closet?

JACK
Half .
Ali picks up the paper, reads an ad.

ALI
Ooh, look! Hot tub!

JACK
Fine. The closet, too.
She weighs it. Makes him suffer. Then:

ALI
Okay.

JACK
Thank you.

ALI
(MOCKING HIM)
Hey, I'm the kind of girl, if a friend's in trouble, I help. That's just who I am.
We HEAR an AUDIENCE laugh O. S. as we...

EXT. BURLESQUE LOUNGE - NIGHT
Small crowd outside.

TESS (O. S.)
So I said to the sailor, I may not be as good as I once was...

INT. BURLESQUE LOUNGE - NIGHT
Through a transparent scrim, the Puccini Triplets perform a sexy harem scene in silhouette, casting larger than life shadows-- Tess walks behind the scrim playfully, in and out of view. The Bumber Band plays off to the side.

TESS
But you can bet your sweet ass I'm better ONCE than I ever was...
The crowd laughs. Tess points to a woman who isn't laughing.

TESS (CONT'D)
Drink up, sister! You're a tad behind.
(to a waiter, re: woman)
Be a dear and bring Mommy over there another scotch.
The crowd chuckles as the Bumper Band kicks in and the harem scene evolves into a sexy tongue-in-cheek silhouetted dance.

INT. BURLESQUE LOUNGE - BACKSTAGE - NIGHT
Tess comes off stage. Sean bustles up to her.

SEAN
The distributor's holding back the booze unless we cut him a check.

TESS
Ply him with drinks, send Scarlett over to flirt, and try to finagle him down to a half.

SEAN
How's a third?
He produces a check, all filled-out, for her to sign.

TESS
Have I told you lately that I love you?

SEAN
Got any brothers?
He bustles off with the check. Scarlett, Coco and Nikki approach the stage wearing leather, strappy Gaultier corsets with gloves and fishnets --post-modern Germanesque -- Nikki is carrying a glass of tequila. Tess eyeballs her--

TESS
Drinking already?

NIKKI
Yes, Mommie.

TESS
You're drunk.

NIKKI
No. But I'm working on it.
Nikki totters a little. Tess looks her over.

TESS
I'm pulling you from this number.
Go home, wring yourself out, and come back tomorrow.

NIKKI
You can't pull me--
Tess SPOTS Ali heading for the dressing room--

TESS
Ali! Take Nikki's spot.

NIKKI
WHAT?! That bitch can't dance my part!

TESS
Ali-- get dressed NOW!
Ali looks at Nikki-- who GLARES at her--

ALI
But, wait-- Tess-- that's always been Nikki's number.
Tess looks at her-- she's really had it with these girls--

TESS
But this is MY club, and now it's your number.
Ali looks between the two of them, Nikki glaring at her--

TESS (CONT'D)
Is there a problem? You said you know the whole show.

(CHALLENGING HER)
You can do anything, right?
Tess just looks at Ali. Nikki stares at Tess, livid, then storms off.

INT. BURLESQUE LOUNGE - SAME
Marcus ENTERS the club and joins Vince at a table. A LOUD

DRUM ROLL. MUSIC UP.
THE STAGE
Ali and the other dancers hit the stage and start in on the vampy "TOUGH LOVER. "
AT THE BAR, Jack is busy mixing drinks. He glances at the stage, then DOUBLE-TAKES on Ali, looking crazy gorgeous. She vamps forward with the girls, they rotate singing into the prop mic.

JESSE
(LIP-SYNCHING)
WELL, I WANT A LOVER WHO MOVES ME
SO_
COCO
(LIP-SYNCHING)
WHO SURE KNOWS HOW TO ROCK N ROLL--
ALI
(LIP-SYNCHING)
I WANT A TOUGH LOVER--
INT. BURLESQUE LOUNGE - SOUND BOOTH - NIGHT
DAVE, the sound guy, looks up as Nikki comes in.

NIKKI
Tess needs you. She said it was urgent.

DAVE
I can't leave here now --

NIKKI
Fine, but don't say I didn't warn you...

DAVE
Shit, okay --
He checks his sound board -- then bolts from the room. Nikki watches him go LOOKS DOWN onto the STAGE as ALI STEPS to

THE MIC--
ALI

(LIP-SYNCHING)
WHEN HE KISSES ME I'LL GET A THRILL, AND WHEN HE DO THAT WIGGLE--

Nikki reaches out and FLIPS A SWITCH.

THE SOUND DROPS OUT. THE PLAYBACK STOPS. The girls freeze in awkward poses, unsure of what to do.

MURMURS in the room as the audience looks around, confused.

BACKSTAGE, Tess looks up at the sound booth, sees it's empty.

Dave appears at her side.

DAVE

You wanted to see me?

ON STAGE -- Ali looks at flustered Tess... the girls... the audience. Panic.

On the floor, Nikki watches with satisfaction as she makes her way over to Marcus. Enjoying the train wreck she caused.

Then -- in a flash, Ali turns to the audience, and SINGS a'capella from the TOP OF THE SONG.

ALI
OH--OH--OOOOOOOOOOH.

She looks around. Silence. Mouths agape. Tess approaches in

THE WINGS--
TESS

(to a stage hand)
Close the Goddman curtain!

SEAN

Hold on...

Ali starts to sing again, her version, slow, and sexy...

ALI
WELL I WANT A LOVER TO MOVE ME SO, WHO SURE KNOWS HOW TO ROCK N ROLL...

Tess looks at Ali, you could knock her over with a feather.

Sean looks at Tess. Scarlett looks at Coco. Jack stares at the stage. Everyone stunned by the sound coming out of this girl. And now the song really takes off!

SUDDENLY, one of the BAND BOYS grabs his sax and plays. Ali jumps in, seamless, as the guys on Bass and Drums join in.

Ali picks up the choreography. The girls fall in with her.

ALI (CONT'D)

I WANT A TOUGH LOVER, YEAH, YEAH. I NEED A TOUGH LOVER. WHOOO. I WANT A TOUGH LOVER. YEAH-YEAH. TOUGH LOVER. UH-HA...

Coco and Scarlett chime in on back-up. Hearing them, Jessie and Anna join in as well. Ali takes off, holding nothing back. The girls feed off her confidence, and soon all of them are hitting the backs of their cabaret chairs, stomping their feet to the music. The girls singing back-up.

In his seat, Marcus sits up a little straighter -- suddenly paying more attention. Unable to take his eyes off Ali.

The BAND plays along. The BARTENDERS accompany them with hand-claps. All except Jack, who's too spellbound to move.

ALI (CONT'D)
WHEN HE KISSES ME I'LL GET A THRILL AND WHEN HE DO THAT WIGGLE, I WON ' T KEEP STILL ...

ON THE FLOOR, Nikki watches, aghast, as the crowd engages like we've never seen them.

ALI/GIRLS
I WANT A TOUGH LOVER, YEAH, YEAH. I NEED A TOUGH LOVER. WHOOO. I WANT A TOUGH LOVER. YEAH-YEAH.
BARTENDERS/GIRLS
TOUGH LOVER. UH-HA...

The girls come alive, finally able to sing a song they've been faking for so long

ALI
THE SEVEN SISTERS GOT NOTHING ON HIM, I 'M TALKING ABOUT A LOVER WHO ' S FAST AS THE WIND. EVER YONE ' LL TALK HOW HE'S GOT ME FIXED, IT AIN'T VOODOO IT'S JUST THAT TWIST.
(MORE)
ALI (CONT'D)
HE'LL BE THE GREATEST LOVER EVER COME TO PASS, DON JUAN AIN'T GOT HALF A CHANCE. HE'LL MAKE ME LAUGH AND HE'LL MAKE ME CRY, HE'LL BE SO TOUGH HE ' LL MAKE VENUS COME ALIVE. HE 'LL DO ANYTHING THAT HE WANTS TO DO, STEP ON JESSIE JAMES' BLUE

SUEDE SHOES.
ALI/GIRLS
I WANT A TOUGH LOVER, YEAH, YEAH. I NEED A TOUGH LOVER. WHOOO. I WANT A TOUGH LOVER. YEAH-YEAH.
BARTENDERS/GIRLS
TOUGH LOVER. UH-HA::!
The room ERUPTS IN APPLAUSE, knowing they caught a once-in-a- lifetime performance. Marcus stands, clapping, whistling.
Ali basks in it, jubilant, rapturous. She glances to the wings and sees Sean, clapping and jumping in place. Then she sees Tess beside him, stone-faced.

INT. BURLESQUE LOUNGE - BACKSTAGE - NIGHT
The Girls exit the stage in a flurry, everyone congratulating Ali -- a whirlwind of hugs, kisses. Ali reaches Tess.

ALI
Tess, when the music stopped--

TESS DAVE
Why didn't you tell me you I have no idea what happened. could blow like that?

ALI (CONT'D)
I did.
Tess spots a TATTOOED BAND GUY in the door.

TESS
Do you boys know all the music?

TATTOOED BAND GUY
Hell, yeah.
Nikki wanders in, drink in hand. Tess looks at them all. Plants her hands on her hips.

TESS
Okay, then. Tomorrow night, Ali sings lead, everyone else is back- up. Questions?
Ali can't keep from beaming as she shakes her head, no!

TESS (CONT'D)
Good.
The Girls file into the dressing room. Tess heads out, past Nikki.

NIKKI
"People don't come to hear us sing. "

TESS
No. But they'll come to hear her sing. Dry out and maybe you can back her up.
She leaves. Nikki scowls. Sean grabs Ali.

SEAN
Bitch, you SANG that damn song!
He heads off to the dressing room, too, leaving Nikki and Ali alone together. Their eyes meet.

NIKKI
One of us has clearly underestimated the other.
She tosses her glass in the trash and leaves Ali alone.

INT. BURLESQUE LOUNGE - NIGHT
Ali trots out from backstage, spots Jack behind the bar. She heads over to him. Before she gets there:

MARCUS
Where'd you learn to sing like that?
She turns. Marcus is there. Handsome, charming and devious as ever.

ALI
You can't learn to sing like that.

MARCUS
Well, you're too good to be singing here.

ALI
I just got into the show and suddenly I'm too good for it?
Shrugs, "but, you are" then--

MARCUS
How about a drink?

ALI
Sure. Jack's at the bar. Tell him I sent you. It's on me.

MARCUS
But I hate lines.
AT THE BAR - Jack looks up, SEES Ali and Marcus talking.

BACK ON MARCUS who looks Ali up and down.

MARCUS (CONT'D)
Seriously. You sound even better than you look. Which is saying a lot.

ALI
Talk about a "line. "
She smiles, amused, and heads away from him, toward the bar.
He watches her go. Tess intercepts Ali.

TESS
What did he want?

ALI
Directions to the bar.
As Ali heads off. Tess glances back at Marcus, mistrustful.

INT. EMPTY BURLESQUE LOUNGE - NIGHT
After hours. The club is closed. Jack, Ali, Coco, Sean and Georgia are sitting around the bar as Jack closes up.

JACK
You blew me away! Who knew you could sing like that?

COCO
Who knew any white chick could sing like that? You channeled that shit.

SEAN
How the hell do you do that, girl?

ALI
I don't know, I can't explain it.
It's like -- I start singing, and something starts to move inside me.
It's in my hands, my feet, my gut,

MY THIGHS
She runs her hands over her body as she describes it. Jack watches her -- holy smokes. Sean notices his gaze on her.

ALI (CONT'D) and it just builds and builds till I feel like I'm gonna explode.

GEORGIA
Trust me, I know what that feels like. I have to pee. Again.

She hops off the stool and scurries to the back. Coco stands, to leave. Looks at Ali.

COCO
Wanna grab something to eat?
Ali looks back at Coco -- validated. Accepted. At last.

ALI
Yeah. Lemme get my bag.
Ali moves off. Coco goes to get her coat. Sean sees Jack still watching Ali as she walks across the room.

SEAN
Well, will you look at that.

JACK
What?

SEAN
You looking at that girl the way I looked at you all those years.
Only difference: you actually stand a chance with her.

JACK
I have a fiancee.

SEAN
Three thousand miles away.

JACK
We talk every day.

SEAN
Let me guess what about: her, her and... oh! Her.
Jack shoots him a glare.

SEAN (CONT'D)
All I'm saying is, this one's beautiful on the inside too. And she won't be on the shelf forever.
Ali comes back, ready to go. Feels them stop talking and look at her.

ALI
What?

SEAN

I was just explaining to Jack that even opportunity has a shelf life.
Jack grabs a trash bag and takes it out back. Sean looks at
Ali more closely. He brushes her hair out of her face. Then he holds it off her shoulders and raises that gay eyebrow.
- INT. SALON - DAY - Ali sits in front of a mirror while Sean gives the HAIRDRESSER very specific instructions.
- INT. JACK'S APARTMENT, AT HIS KEYBOARD, Jack plays a high- energy style piano which runs over a QUICK SEQUENCE: It's the instrumental music to: "BUT I'M A GOOD GIRL. "
- INT. BURLESQUE LOUNGE - The Burlesque Girls dance on stage, performing a high-energy tap dance, coupled with a European slap-dance, with the slapping of each other's bodies and faces integrated with tapping and music. It's very cabaret, but modernized with contemporary STEPPING. CARRY MUSIC:
- INT. SALON - LATER - The HAIRDRESSER spins the chair around. Ali's her hair is platinum blonde, with bangs and a
Louise Brooks bob that frames her face beautifully. Her smoky eyes pop like never before. Ali studies herself:

ALI
Where have I been all my life?

- INT. BURLESQUE LOUNGE - NIGHT - CAMERA MOVES OVER THE
AUDIENCE, the brass section kicks in giving the piano a
BIGGER, BAWDY, SHOW-STOPPING BOISTEROUS SOUND as Ali APPEARS with her new look. Amazing. Like Helmut Newton meets Carnaby
St. circa 1 As she begins this HIGH ENERGY SONG-- Jack is looks up from the bar. Totally blown away.

ALI (CONT'D)
THE DRESS IS BOHAN. THE SHOES ARE JOURDAN. THE BAG NORTH AFRICAN, AND SO IS THE TAN. MY ADDRESS TODAY, FABER ST. HONERE, TOMORROW RIO, THE CONCORDE THE WAY. MY RING IS BULGARI, IT MAKES THEIR HEADS TWIRL, THEY ALL SAY, 'DARLING, WHAT DID YOU DO FOR THAT PEARL?' WHAT? I AM A GOOD GIRL. NEW YORK CREON, COTE D 'AZUR. L. A. POLO LOUNGE, FOR BREAKFAST FOR SURE. PARIS, LA PLAZA, OR MAYBE THE RITZ. IN LONDON THE PLAYBOY, IN TRUTH IT'S THE PITS. YOU KNOW I HAVE FOUND, THE

WORD ' S GONE AROUND. THEY ALL SAY MY FEET NEVER DO TOUCH THE GROUND.
WHAT?. I AM A GOOD GIRL.

Ali finishes the song to big applause. Takes her bow. Makes her way off the stage and ACROSS the club to...

JACK AT THE BAR - he turns to see Ali.

ALI (CONT'D)

Hiya, big boy.

She spins herself around on a bar stool, so he can see all angles. Jack likes plenty. Way too much.

ALI (CONT'D)

What do you think?

JACK

(FLUSTERED)

It's... I think-you look... I mean, yeah... do you like it?

Not the reaction she was looking for.

ALI

Jack. It's okay for you to think I look hot. We're friends for chrissakes. It's not like we're brother and sister.

She rolls her eyes, gets up, and heads backstage. Jack watches her go--

JACK

(TO HIMSELF)

No. We certainly are not.

INT. BURLESQUE LOUNGE - BACKSTAGE - NIGHT

The Burlesque Girls are prepping for the show.

NIKKI

Why the hell is everyone having a conniption over her? She's just a tacky, pushy girl from a --

Ali -- sexy, sophisticated, gorgeous -- enters.

NIKKI (CONT'D)

-- fly-over state.

Ali pretends she didn't hear. She sits at her mirror. The girls stare at her, mouths agape. Ali picks up her mascara wand, looks down the mirror at Nikki's reflection.

ALI

(FAUX INNOCENT)
What's a fly-over state?
Ali takes a deft stroke of her wand over her lashes, then bats them at Nikki. Nikki walks out. Coco smiles with appreciation. Whistles long and low. The girls all laugh.

INT. BURLESQUE LOUNGE - NIGHT
Tess glad-hands guests, then spots Vince, waving at her. She starts over, then sees Marcus in the booth with Vince. She turns and walks the other way. Vince catches up to her.

VINCE
TESS --
TESS
Vince, if I were going to sell, I'd have sold to those idiots building that monstrosity across the street.
I said no.

VINCE
Which made Marcus bump his offer up again. It's obscene, what he wants to give us. At least hear him out.

INT. BURLESQUE LOUNGE - TESS'S CLUTTERED OFFICE - NIGHT
Tess, at her desk, reads a contract. Marcus and Vince sit across from her, watching.

MARCUS
It's very simple. I buy you out and pay you a million off the top.
(motions to Vince)
Five hundred grand each.
Tess looks up from the contract, squints at Marcus.

TESS
Why do you want this club so badly?

MARCUS
Best view on the Sunset Strip.

VINCE
Do you know what you could do with that money, Tess?

TESS
Do you know what you can do with that money, Vince?

VINCE

Be reasonable. We're rolling vendors ninety days out.

MARCUS
The club's not even worth what you paid for it. You've got a second mortgage, you can't get a third.
Tess looks at Vince, betrayed.

TESS
Did you also tell him about the tattoo on my ass?

VINCE
It's business, Tess. Not personal.

TESS
My business. Which I built from the ground up.

MARCUS
You're not gonna get another opportunity like this.

TESS
Exactly.
She looks at a photo on her wall: the Burlesque Girls, in all their glory.

TESS (CONT'D)
Which is why I'll never let it go.
She gets up, opens the door, ushering them out. Marcus shoots Vince an angry look as they head downstairs.
IN THE STAIRWELL, Vince reassures Marcus:

VINCE
Don't worry. The balloon payment's due on the first. She doesn't have the money. She has to sell.
IN TESS'S OFFICE, Tess stands in the doorway, having heard.
Then she walks back to her desk and sits, dejected. Head in her hands. For the first time ever, looking worried and defeated. Something she'd never show anyone. A beat. Then:

SEAN
Well. We've had a pretty good run.
She looks up. Sean is in the doorway.

SEAN (CONT'D)
Maybe it's time to just... hang it up. Let it go. Call it a day.
Tess's eyes go steely with determination.

TESS
No. You cannot say that to me. I can eat these "sky is falling" dipshits for breakfast, lunch, and dinner, but not YOU. You cannot be that person. I've scoured dirty flea markets for costumes, stayed up all night sewing till my fingers bled, painted and repainted every goddamn wall of this place myself.

(MORE)
TESS (CONT'D)
I choreographed every step of every number. I've played nursemaid, sister, mother and shrink to every girl who's ever danced here. I've hocked every keepsake I've ever owned to keep this place afloat.
Because this club is the last of it's kind, and if it goes away, one day there won't be anything like it-
- and THAT would be a tragedy. So you cannot say that to me. Because now someone's gotta believe in me,
Goddamnit. And I need that person to be you. So don't you ever let me hear you say that again. I will never let this club go. Never.
Sean looks at her... a wry smile.

SEAN
There she is. Thought I'd lost you for a minute.
Tess just looks at him, and smiles. He grabs a boa, throws it around his neck and exits. When he's gone, Tess's smile fades.
IN THE CLUB, the place is empty. Jack is wiping down the bar cleaning up. He starts stacking some chairs in the house as. . SEAN CROSSES the floor.

SEAN (CONT'D)
Night, Jack.

JACK
Night.
Sean EXITS as Jack carries a stack of chairs to the side of the room, sets them down near the piano. STOPS, grabs a chair for himself and sits down. Begins to play an original song.
ACROSS THE ROOM, Ali ENTERS from backstage. Her dance bag over her shoulder. She HEARS the piano, peers around a column, SEES Jack playing. She stays in the shadows and watches as he sings and plays a beautiful song. (TBD)
The song ends. Ali applauds slowly. Impressed. Jack looks up, surprised that she is there.

ALI
Beautiful. You write that?

JACK
Just some sentimental crap. Ready?
She smiles at his modesty. Nods. He crosses to her. Grabs her dance bag and they EXIT together.

INT. JACK'S APARTMENT - LATE AFTERNOON
Jack enters, unloading his keyboard from his back. He hears
Ali in the bedroom. He quietly moves over to the ajar bedroom door -- peeks in and sees:
ALI, in bra and undies. She hums the song he played the night before in the mirror as she gets dressed.
ON JACK, watching, mesmerized. His eyes travel her body.
She moves out of view. He leans against the wall to try to keep seeing her -- and steps on the CAT. It MEOWS. He flattens against the wall. Ali looks up.

ALI
Jack?
Jack zips back to the door, opens it quietly, then SLAMS it.

JACK
Hey! Just got home!
Ali grabs a dress from her bed, slips into it.

ALI
In here! Can you zip me up?
In a nanosecond-- Jack enters the bedroom.

ALI (CONT'D)
Hey. Where you been?

JACK
Rehearsing. I'm playing a late show tonight.
As he zips up the back of her dress, he sees the PHOTO propped against the lamp on the bedside table.

JACK (CONT'D)
Who is that?
She picks up the picture. Looks at it.

ALI
Me and my mom on my 7th birthday.
She died just a few weeks later.

JACK

She was so young.

ALI
There was so much she never got to do. Sometimes I feel like, if I make the most of my life, part of her will get to live a little more, too.

JACK
Wow. You must miss her.
She puts the photo down. Turns back to him. They're close.

ALI
Every single day, something happens
I want to tell her about.

JACK
What was today's?
A beat. Their eyes connect.

ALI
Don't know. Hasn't happened yet.
They stand there, close to each other. Jack sees a strand of hair caught in the earring. He pulls it away, freeing it.
His fingers move through her hair. She closes her eyes, feeling his fingers against her neck.
Then she opens her eyes, looks at him. He looks back, unable to look away. Until:
His CELL PHONE RINGS. Breaking the mood. He pulls it from his pocket. Checks who's calling. Looks back at Ali.

JACK
I should... it's... Natalie.
Ali steps away from him, disappointed. He answers the phone.

JACK (CONT'D)
Hey, babe, how are you?
Ali watches him walk away from her, falling into the conversation with Natalie.

JACK (CONT'D)
Yes, she's still here-What do you want me to do, it's not like you're here helping out, you know...
Ali grabs her bag and jacket, heads for the door.
MUSIC UP: An incredibly sexy saxophone which takes us to:
FULL CLOSE UP: ALI steps into frame, starts singing.

ALI
A GUY WHAT TAKES HIS TIME...
PULL BACK to reveal she's on stage at the club with the BURLESQUE GIRLS. Finger waves and 1920's sexy clothes.

ALI (CONT'D)
I'LL GO FOR ANY TIME. I'M A FAST MOVIN' GAL WHO LIKES THEM SLOW. GOT NO USE FOR FANCY DRIVIN', WANT TO SEE A GUY ARRIVIN' IN LOW. I'D BE SATISFIED TO KNOW A GUY WHAT TAKES HIS TIME...
THE SONG CONTINUES OVER:
- INT. JACK'S LIVING ROOM - Ali lies on her stomach on the floor perusing a Fashion Magazine. Across the room, Jack sits on the couch, PLAYING HIS KEYBOARD--UNDERSCORING THE SONG. He looks at Ali. Watching her. Without looking up, she takes a pencil, gathers her hair, and puts it up expertly. A few strands fall back onto her neck. Sexy. Ali feels his stare.
Looks up at him. Smiles. He smiles back. She goes back to her magazine. ON JACK. Loving that she's there.
- INT. BURLESQUE LOUNGE - DRESSING ROOM - Ali, the Girls and Sean getting ready. Georgia bursts into the room, showing off an ENGAGEMENT RING. Everyone jumps up, congratulates her.
- INT. BURLESQUE STAGE - The GIRLS and Ali vamp, singing:

ALI (CONT'D)
A GUY WHAT TAKES HIS TIME, I'D GO FOR ANYTIME. A HASTY JOB REALLY SPOILS A MASTER'S TOUCH ...
AT THE BAR, Jack watches as he pours drinks.
- EXT. STREET. AFTERNOON - Ali on the back of Jack's motorcycle, puts her arms around his waist. Jack revs the engine. Weaving through traffic on the Strip. The wind in their hair. Her scarf tears away, lifting into the air...
- INT. BURLESQUE STAGE - Ali and Burlesque girls continue...

ALI (CONT'D)
I DON'T LIKE A BIG COMMOTION, I'M A DEMON FOR SLOW MOTION OR SUCH. WHY SHOULD I DENY, THAT I WOULD DIE, TO KNOW A GUY WHAT TAKES HIS TIME ...
- INT. JACK'S LIVING ROOM - Ali, Sean, Tess, Scarlett, Anna,

Georgia, DAMON (her fiance), hanging out in the living room, decorated with party gear. The lights dim and Jack and Coco enter with a birthday cake. They set it in front of Ali.
Ali looks around at her friends, drinking it in. She locks eyes with Jack -- then closes her eyes and BLOWS.
- INT. BURLESQUE STAGE - Ali, still singing her song.

ALI (CONT'D)
I CAN SPOT AN AMATEUR, APPRECIATE A CONNOISSEUR IN HIS TRADE, WHO WOULD QUALIFY, NO ALIBI, TO BE THE GUY, WHO TAKES HIS TIME...
PULL BACK to reveal A PACKED HOUSE. The audience goes nuts.
Marcus is at his table, clapping, whistling, her biggest fan.

INT. BURLESQUE LOUNGE - AT THE BAR - LATER
Ali walks up to the bar.

ALI
Hey -- when can you cut out? I'm about to fall asleep standing up.

JACK
I have that gig, remember? In fact, I gotta head out or I'm gonna be late.
(checking his watch)
I can maybe swing you home before.

ALI
No, that's okay, you go. I'll grab a ride with Coco.
He grabs his jacket from under the bar. As he heads out:

JACK
By the way -- you killed.

ALI
(looks at him, smiles)
Thanks.
He disappears out the back exit. Ali turns around and finds herself face to face with Marcus.

MARCUS
You ready?

ALI

For what?

MARCUS
I'll drop you off.

(BEAT)
Coco left five minutes ago.
She realizes he was listening to her conversation.

ALI
Excuse me?

MARCUS
Sorry-- I was coming to talk to you and caught the end of your conversation.

ALI
(putting on her coat reaching for her bags)
Talk to me about... ?

MARCUS
Dinner. With me. Gimmie that.
He swoops down and GRABS her dance bag and purse, turns and heads out.

MARCUS (CONT'D)
(WALKING AWAY)
If you ever expect to see this bag alive again... you'll come with me.

ALI
Hey... ! Come back here... !

INT. MARCUS'S BENTLEY - NIGHT
ON Ali, looking out the window with her arms crossed. WIDEN to REVEAL, she's in car with Marcus, zipping along Sunset.

ALI
Where are you taking me?

MARCUS
I told you-- to dinner.

ALI
Dinner? What about Nikki-- What's up with you and Nikki?

MARCUS
We're friends.

ALI
Where I'm from friends don't chew each other's earlobes.

MARCUS
Aren't you glad you left?
(then, remembering)
Oh, damn!

ALI
What?

MARCUS
I just remembered I have to make a quick appearance at a party.

ALI
You just remembered.

MARCUS
It's on the way. We'll be quick.
Ten minutes, tops. Do you mind?

ALI
And if I do.

MARCUS
Then you've been kidnapped.
He turns off Sunset and heads up into the hills.

EXT. MODERN HOUSE - HOLLYWOOD HILLS - NIGHT
Sprawling 60's modern. Walls of glass. Jetliner views.
Valets running around out front.

INT. MODERN HOUSE - HOLLYWOOD HILLS - NIGHT
Fabulous party underway. Packed with glitterati. Music blares, caterers weave through the hip crowd. Marcus leads
Ali in and guides her through the crowd.

ALI
Wow. Nice house.

PARTY GUEST
Hey, Marcus --

MARCUS
Hey, how you doing?
He shakes the guy's hand and moves on through the party.
Someone else calls out to him.

ANOTHER GUEST
Marcus!

MARCUS
Hey, let me get a drink, I'll be

BACK --
Marcus pulls Ali in the opposite direction, avoiding another
GROUP trying to greet him. He grabs two wine glasses off a tray, gives one to Ali, then pushes through a door into:

INT. MODERN HOUSE - KITCHEN - NIGHT
Bustling, food and booze everywhere. Marcus spots several trays of hors d'oeuvres. He picks up two of them.

ALI
Marcus -- you can't just take that.

MARCUS
SHHH --
He hands her one tray, sticks a bottle of wine in one pocket, throws an opener in another.

ALI
They're gonna throw us out of here.

MARCUS
Not if we sneak out first, come on.
He kicks open a back door.

EXT. MODERN HOUSE - BACK YARD - NIGHT
A sky full of stars, hovering over an expansive back yard.
Music from the party drifts out. Marcus looks around, up --

MARCUS
Up there.

He starts up some steps to an outdoor gazebo. Ali follows.
They pass AN INCREDIBLY WELL-DRESSED COUPLE coming down.

GUY
Hey, Marcus --

MARCUS
Hey, Guys. Greg, Marla, this is
Ali.
They exchange hellos. Ali notices:

ALI
Ooh. Killer shoes.

MARLA
Aren't they? Louboutins.

GREG
(TO MARCUS)
Great party, as always.

MARCUS
Glad you could come.
Ali stares at Marcus. He smiles, takes her hand, keeps leading her up the stairs.

AL I
You had to make an appearance at your own party?

MARCUS
Would've been rude not to, right?
You'd like those guys. Greg's the entertainment editor at the Times, and Marla's a designer.
Ali glances back at Marla again, locks in on her shoes.

AL I
I'm gonna dream about those shoes.

MARCUS
Thousand dollars a pop.

AL I
Jesus. Who can afford that?

MARCUS
I can.

ALI
Hey, I saw them first.
He laughs as they reach the top of the stairs and a
BREATHTAKING PANORAMIC VIEW OF THE ENTIRE CITY is revealed.
Ali pauses, taking in the glittering, massive view of L. A.

ALI (CONT'D)
Whoa. L. A. looks one hell of a lot prettier from up here.

MARCUS
It should. That view cost me three times what the house did.

(POINTING)
See that strip mall down there?

ALI
You own that too?

MARCUS
No. I own everything above it.

ALI
There is nothing above it.

MARCUS
Exactly.

ALI
You own... air?

MARCUS
Air rights. The guy who owns the strip mall was having money issues and almost had to sell. Whoever he sold to would have put in a huge tower. So I bought the air rights.
Now no one can ever build above one story.

ALI
Aren't you the sly puss.

MARCUS
Mall guy gets to keep his property.

I get to keep the second best view in L. A.

ALI
What's the first?
He gazes at her. She rolls her eyes.

ALI (CONT'D)
How many girls have you used that on?

MARCUS
None who ever called me on it.
He smiles. Looks at her. Then...

MARCUS (CONT'D)
What do you want, Ali? In life.
Girl like you, gives up everything, gets on a bus heading for total uncertainty-- she's got a dream. I want to know what it is.

ALI
Why?

MARCUS
Because you're talented enough to get whatever you want. And I'm smart enough to help make it happen. So? What do you want?
A beat. She thinks about it. Looks him in the eye.

ALI
I want to be the best singer I can be. I want to give as much joy as I get when I perform. And I want to die knowing I made the most of every opportunity life gave me.

MARCUS
That's ... so beautiful.

AL I
There wasn't a dry eye in the house when I said it at the Grundy County
Junior Miss Talent Show.
His eyes narrow.

MARCUS
Why do you women always take advantage of nice boys?

ALI
Oh, please. You are SO not a nice boy.

He clinks her glass. Smiles at her. Devilish and sexy.

INT. MARCUS'S HOUSE - WEE HOURS - NIGHT
Party's over. Lights low. Ali walks through the almost- empty house, passes a COUPLE making out on a couch, a GUY who holds out a joint. She motions "no thanks", heads into the:
LIVING ROOM, where Marcus is asleep on a Bertolli chair, drink in hand. An OLDER GUY is playing the piano quietly.
Ali takes the drink from Marcus's hand, sets it on the table.
She hears the pianist start a new song: (TBD). She smiles.
Goes over to him.

ALI
Ooh, I love this song.
The Piano Player scoots to make room. She sits beside him. He starts humming along. She does too. Then he sings a line.
She sings one back. And they fall in together. Not vamping, not performing. Just feeling the beauty of the music in the middle of the night.

INT. JACK'S APARTMENT - NIGHT - CARRY MUSIC
Jack quietly lets himself in. He sets his keyboard down, then sees the bedroom door cracked, the light on.

JACK
Ali?
He looks in. Empty. He checks the clock: 4: He hears a
"meow", and sees the cat. He picks it up, turns out the light, and leaves the room.

INT. BURLESQUE LOUNGE - BACKSTAGE - NIGHT
Sean, Coco, Nikki, Jesse, and the rest of the girls in early stages of getting ready. Ali enters.

COCO
Someone has a package!
Ali sees A GIFT BOX at her station. She reads the card: "You saw them first. " She opens the box and sees the Louboutins.

JESSE
Ooh. Faboo.
Nikki picks one up -- checking their authenticity.

NIKKI
Who's the sucker?

All eyes turn to Ali. She's saved by Tess entering.

TESS
Coco-puff, shake a leg, you're on in five, Georgie-Girl, Ali-Cat -- move, move, move --
Tess exits.

ALI
Ahh. My Nanna used to call me her
Ali-Cat.

SEAN
Yet another fascinating story.

NIKKI
Why doesn't Tess have a nickname for me?

COCO
Oh, she does.
A knowing look amongst the girls.

NIKKI
She never uses it.

SEAN
Sure she does.

NIKKI
When?

SEAN
Just after you leave the room.
Nikki gives him the finger and walks out. A beat. Then:

GIRLS TOGETHER
Coke-whore.
They crack up. CUE MUSIC: "STRANGE THINGS HAPPENING"

INT. BURLESQUE LOUNGE - ON STAGE - NIGHT
Ali and the Burlesque Girls vamp forward and perform "STRANGE
THINGS HAPPENING", a decadent, rockin' dance/singing number.
Scantily-clad girls pose and dance on chairs with images projected onto them -- a rock fantasy with burlesque moves
(like Bob Fosse's "All That Jazz")

ALI
WELL I STAY OUT LATE AT NIGHT. I DON'T TREAT MY BABY RIGHT. THERE'S STRANGE THINGS HAPPENING EVERY DAY...
MUSIC CONTINUES OVER:
- INT. JACK'S APARTMENT - Jack, playing his keyboards. Ali comes in, wearing the Louboutins.

JACK
You were out late last night.

ALI
I got a ride home with that guy--
Marcus-- we went to a party. It was fun.

JACK
Marcus the Asshole?

ALI
Yeah. Turns out he's not so bad.
She heads past him, toward the kitchen. He notices:

JACK
New shoes?

- INT. BURLESQUE LOUNGE - ON STAGE - NIGHT
Ali, singing. Marcus in the audience, watching her.

ALI
THE LOVE THAT YOU REFUSE, SOME OTHER GUY CAN USE, STRANGE THINGS ARE HAPPENING EVERY DAY ...
- INT. BURLESQUE LOUNGE - NIGHT
Ali performing. Marcus watching from his table. With him is GREG (from the party). Jack watches from the bar.

ALI (O. S.) (CONT'D)
OOH EVERY DAY ...
All the Bartenders sing, except Jack, who keeps his eyes on Marcus.

BARTENDERS
EVERY DAY!
ALI
EVERY DAY. ' THERE ' S STRANGE THINGS
HAPPENING EVERY DAY ...
- INT. JACK'S APARTMENT - DAY
Ali getting dressed to go out. She's wearing the Louboutins, crossing back and forth in front of Jack, who's on the sofa.

JACK
There's only one reason a man buys a woman shoes, you know.

ALI
So what if I'm getting a little male attention.

JACK
You get a lot more than a little.

ALI
Not from anyone who matters.

JACK
(CLEARLY IRRITATED)
I just think that you should be careful.
Ali stops in front of him. Hands on her hips.

AL I
And I just think that -- if you really feel the need to tell a girl what she should and shouldn't do, you should pick up the phone and call your fiancee.

- INT. BURLESQUE LOUNGE - NIGHT
Ali continues to sing.

ALI (CONT'D)
WELL, I'D NEVER MISS MY WATER,
UNTIL MY WELL RUNS DRY...
AT THEIR TABLE, Greg leans into Marcus and whispers something, impressed. Marcus nods back: "Told you. "

ALI (CONT'D)
STRANGE THINGS HAPPENING EVERY DAY.
- EXT. HOLLYWOOD HILLS - NIGHT
Marcus drives Ali up the windy roads, into the hills.

They're talking animatedly.

ALI (O. S.) (CONT'D)
. THEY WON'T BE SATISFIED, 'TIL
THEY SEE TEARDROPS IN MY EYES ...
- INT. JACK'S APARTMENT - NIGHT
Jack staring at a note: "Jack: going out, see you tom'w. - A"

ALI (O. S.) (CONT'D)
STRANGE THINGS ARE HAPPENING
EVERY DAY.
- INT. BURLESQUE STAGE - NIGHT
Ali moves in sync with the Girls. Tess watches from the wings, pleased.

ALI (CONT'D)
STRANGE THINGS ARE HAPPENING EVERY
DAY, OOH EVERY DAY!
BARTENDERS
EVERY DAY!
ALI
EVERY DAY. THERE ' S STRANGE THINGS
HAPPENING EVERY DAY ...
- INT. FABULOUS PARTY - NIGHT
Marcus leads Ali through a party, introducing her to everyone, making sure she knows people and is known by them.

ALI (O. S.) (CONT'D)
WELL YOU THOUGHT I WAS A FOOL, BUT
I GOT NEWS FOR YOU ... STRANGE
THINGS ARE HAPPENING EVERY DAY.
- INT. BURLESQUE LOUNGE - NIGHT
Nikki watches from the wings, seething, as Marcus delights in Ali's performance.

ALI (CONT'D)
I THINK I FOUND SOMEONE NEW ...
- INT. JACK'S APARTMENT - NIGHT
Wee hours. Ali comes in, shuts the door as quietly as she can, then tiptoes past Jack, asleep on the couch.

ALI (O. S.) (CONT'D)
AND I THINK IT'S THROUGH WITH
YOU...

After she passes... Jack's eyes open.

- INT. BURLESQUE LOUNGE - NIGHT
Ali, owning the stage and the room.

ALI (CONT'D)
STRANGE THINGS ARE HAPPENING EVERY DAY ... YEAAAAAHHH: STRANGE THINGS ARE HAPPENING!! HAPPENING . 1
The SONG ENDS in a flourish. There's a CAMERA FLASH!
FREEZE FRAME on the image: ALI, belting onstage, with the Burlesque Girls striking a pose behind her.
WIDEN to see it's a photo on the front page of the L. A. TIMES Calendar section. The headline: "BURLESQUE HAS A VOICE:".

INT. JACK'S APARTMENT - MORNING
Jack, sleepy, in boxers, stares at the newspaper, bewildered.

JACK
Hey. Have you seen this?

ALI
What?
Ali wanders out of the bathroom, brushing her teeth. He shows her the paper. She SCREAMS.

INT. BURLESQUE LOUNGE - BACKSTAGE - AFTERNOON
The Burlesque Girls (minus Ali) crowd around the paper.

NIKKI
That's bullshit.

SCARLETT
No. That's major.

NIKKI
(pointing to photo)
Look again. The only thing major is the size of your ass.
Nikki walks off-- Scarlett pick up the paper, looks closer--
Ali enters, dance bag over her shoulder, running late. The Burlesque Girls and Sean all APPLAUD (except Nikki) Ali smiles. Embarrassed. She curtsies sarcastically.
Coco points to a BOUQUET OF ROSES at Ali's station.

COCO
From Monsieur Louboutin, I presume.
Ali reads the card: "To the best view in L. A. - M". Sean shoves her down in her seat, pulls her coat off.

SEAN
Shake your tail, Alicat, you still got a show to do.

EXT. THE BURLESQUE LOUNGE - NIGHT
A PACKED LINE of chattering hipsters snakes down the block.

MUSIC UP: "JUNGLE FEVER" BY THE CHAKACHAS. (REVAMPED BERLIN MUSIC)
INT. BURLESQUE LOUNGE - ON STAGE - NIGHT
Daredevils Missy and Kitten DeVille, in striped stockings, corsets, and tons of cleavage, swing on a trapeze over the audience. Playing the comedy, grabbing each other in all the right places. Classic Burlesque, unusually bawdy. Equally suggestive, funny, and skillful.
Tess, all dolled-up, weaves through the tables, greeting, welcoming, reveling in the crowd.
FIND Ali as she strides over to Marcus's booth. He stands, hands her a glass of champagne.

MARCUS
To the girl of the hour.

ALI
I'm starting to think you'll go to any length.

MARCUS
(INNOCENTLY)
I just made a call to Greg at the
Times.

ALI
Well-- I appreciate the kudos.
(re: crowded room)
And Tess appreciates the business.

MARCUS
This has NOTHING to do with Tess.
This is about you. And me.

ALI
You are so full of it.
He laughs-- takes her arm--

MARCUS
I've got another friend I want you to meet.
She sees HAROLD SAINT sitting in the booth. He's in his 60's, still dressing like Robert Evans in his heyday.

MARCUS (CONT'D)
Ali Rose, Harold Saint.

ALI
(SHOCKED)
Harold Saint? Shut up. You worked with Etta James.

HAROLD
Her, she chewed me up and spat me out, that one. But with her voice, I forgive her everything.

(THEN)
You got a set of pipes on you, too, little girl. I like your sound.

ALI
Thank you.

(SMILES)
I like yours.

HAROLD
You ever recorded?

ALI
Not yet.

HAROLD
We should do something about that.
He stands. Turns to Marcus.

HAROLD (CONT'D)
See you round, kiddo.
He points his finger, gun-style, which would seem cheesy, but he's old school, so instead it's weirdly cool. He leaves.

ALI
Holy shit. Harold Saint.
AT THE BAR, Jack watches Ali and Marcus talking excitedly.
Not liking what he sees. Sean breezes by, grabs a drink.

SEAN
You snooze, you lose, pretty boy.

INT. BURLESQUE LOUNGE - BACKSTAGE - NIGHT
Sean grips the drink in his teeth as he bustles through the backstage, gathering costumes. He passes Tess going the other way.

TESS
Can you believe this crowd?
He dumps the costumes in her arms.

SEAN
'bout time. These poor babies are begging for your glue-gun.
Tess walks off with the armful of clothes, so happy, humming to herself, passes her OFFICE-- OPENS the door to SEE--
VINCE is sitting at her desk. He flinches at the sight of her-

TESS
Can you believe the crowd out there? Never thought I'd see-
She stops in her tracks, spotting Vince's PANTS on the FLOOR, and a TRAIL OF WOMEN'S CLOTHES to...
THE NEW COCKTAIL WAITRESS, peering out, half-dressed, from behind the curtains--

TESS (CONT'D)
(DISGUSTED)
In my god damn office?
She shakes her head-- GRABS HER PURSE-- and walks out.

EXT. BURLESQUE LOUNGE - PARKING LOT - NIGHT
Tess, pissed off, carries the damaged costumes out to her car. Nikki is behind her, following her out.

NIKKI
Tess. We need to talk.
Tess rolls her eyes, doesn't slow.

TESS
Not now, Nikki.

NIKKI
Yes, now. I've been here since the beginning. We built this club together. And then some girl shows up out of nowhere-- who hasn't even paid her dues--

TESS
I'll get her to write a check tomorrow.

NIKKI
And suddenly it's her show?

TESS
No, it's not her show. It's my show. But people want to hear her sing. She's bringing them in off the streets. You better believe I'm building a show around her!

NIKKI
I can sing too! And you know it.
But you don't give a shit. You always say this is a dance troupe, now suddenly it's not?

TESS
NIKKI--
NIKKI
And you expect me to dance behind a girl who struts in with a new pair of shoes she got for sleeping with
Marcus Gerber?

TESS
(unlocking her car)
Nikki, you're wasted. Go home.

NIKKI
I won't be upstaged by some slut with mutant lungs!
Tess hurls the costumes in the trunk of her car, furious.

TESS
So don't be! Leave! If you don't want to be a part of what's happening here, then I don't want you around.

NIKKI
(AGHASST)
You'd destroy our friendship and break up the group over some girl you barely know?

TESS
Since when do you care about friendship? Or this group? You're a trainwreck, Nikki! You put tequila on your breakfast cereal!
I'm struggling to survive here, and you show up too drunk to dance!
You call that loyalty?
Nikki just looks at her--

NIKKI
Okay, then. I quit!
Nikki stomps off. Tess sighs --

TESS
NIKKI-- WAIT--
NIKKI
Marcus says you're losing the club anyway!

(MOCKING HER)
"They don't come to hear us sing"

(MORE)
NIKKI (CONT'D)
(SOTTO)
Stupid bitch.
Nikki flips her off and keeps walking. Then turns once more:

NIKKI (CONT'D)
By the way: I slept with Vince the day after your honeymoon.
Tess's eyes narrow. She grabs a HIGH-HEELED PUMP and HURLS it. It flies through the air and hits Nikki in the back of the head. Nikki SCREAMS, whips around, incredulous, to see:
TESS, running right at her. Nikki bolts, heading for her car. She jumps in, locks the door just as Tess SMASHES her fist on the window and KICKS the door. Nikki starts the car.

NIKKI (CONT'D)
You crazy bitch!
Nikki screeches off, leaving Tess alone in the parking lot.
Tess stands there a moment, then HEADS back into the club.

INT. BURLESQUE LOUNGE - NIGHT
The club is totally empty. Everyone is gone. Tess ENTERS,
GRABS her bag as she spots a cabaret chair lying on it's side on stage. She crosses onto the stage. Picks up the chair as...

DAVE (O. S.)
Night, Tess.
Tess looks up, Dave is closing up the sound booth.

TESS
Night, Dave.
Dave FLIPS a big lever, and almost all the lights go OUT, leaving one shaft of light across the stage. We HEAR Dave leave, as the street door closes shut. Tess alone on stage.

BEGIN TESS SOLO SONG NUMBER. TO BE WRITTEN.
INT. JACK'S APARTMENT - NIGHT
Ali enters quietly, all dressed up. She slips off her heels and tiptoes to the bedroom. She slowly opens the bedroom door, then stops when she sees:
JACK, asleep in the bed. Ali looks at him, then looks at the couch. Empty. She closes the door, fluffs the pillow, lies down on the couch, and pulls the blankets up over her.
She lies in the darkness. PUSH THROUGH the wall to see Jack, lying awake in the bed, the cat on his lap.

EXT. LOS ANGELES - WIDE PANORAMA - MORNING
THE SOUND OF A COFFEE GRINDER
INT. JACK'S APARTMENT - MORNING
CLOSE ON Ali, sleeping on the sofa-- abruptly wakes to the deafening grinding of coffee. She gets up, drags herself to the kitchen. Sees Jack, grinding the coffee way longer than is necessary.

ALI
You really need to do that at 6 in the morning?
He turns, sees her.

JACK
Little overdressed for breakfast.

ALI
My pajamas were in my bedroom.
Which was occupied.

JACK
Well, you're never here so... it's stupid for me to crash on the couch every night when there's a perfectly good empty bed.
Jack grinds the coffee beans again. Ali winces.

ALI
So -- you want the bedroom back?
Is that what you're saying?

JACK
The bed should be used by someone.

ALI
Hey, I'm home every night. Maybe not when you think I should be, but last I checked, you were my roommate, not my mother.

(MORE)
99
ALI (CONT'D)
However, since it's an issue, what the hell, take the bed, I'll sleep on the sofa. I don't care.

JACK
Fine.

ALI
Fine.

JACK
You'll have to move all your shit.

ALI
I realize that.

JACK
Cause the room's a total mess --

ALI
I'll move my stuff, God --

JACK
Clothes, make-up, shoes, hair things.

ALI
Jesus, Jack, what is your problem?
Ever since I started hanging out with Marcus, you've been acting like a class-A prick. Is there something you want to say?

JACK

What? No. What do I care? You're ambitious, he can make things happen, go ahead, make a deal with the devil, what's it to me?

ALI
First of all: He's not the devil.
He's a smart businessman. And oddly enough-- a gentleman.

(JACK SCOFFS)
Second: I'm gonna take the couch, and you're gonna 86 the attitude.
Or I'm finding another place to live.
She storms out of the kitchen, tripping over the cat-- a LOUD MEOW! as the cat scurries away, Jack intercepting him--

JACK
And try not to kill the cat!
A SLAM of the bedroom door. MUSIC UP: INSTRUMENTAL to "BABY IT'S YOUR by The Shirelles.

EXT. SUNSET TOWER HOTEL - NIGHT - CARRY MUSIC
CLOSE ON: A DIAMOND RING as it's placed on the hand of A VERY PREGNANT GEORGIA. Wearing an adorable mini-skirt maternity wedding dress. She looks at DAMON with devotion.
Ali, Tess, Coco, Sean and Jack, all watching the ceremony.
Ali looks over at Jack. He looks at her, then away.

EXT. SUNSET TOWER HOTEL - NIGHT - CARRY MUSIC
The reception is underway. GUESTS are drinking, dancing with the iconic backdrop of Hollywood behind them. Ali, Sean,
Coco and Tess stand together drinking, overlooking the city.
ACROSS THE TERRACE, Jack is talking on his cell phone.

JACK
What do you mean, you're still in
New York? ... So you just -- decided not to come? You think you might've wanted to, I don't know, let me know??? We haven't seen each other in six months.
ACROSS THE TERRACE, Ali sees Jack yelling into his phone.
Sean sees her watching.

BACK ON JACK
JACK (CONT'D)
. why does every conversation we have end up being about YOUR future...
Jack looks across the terrace at Ali. Moonlight on her shoulders. A breeze in her hair.

JACK (CONT'D)
. you know what, you're right. We both should be thinking about our futures. And I might just be looking at mine right now. Break a leg baby.
Jack hangs up with finality and marches toward the bar-- His cell phone immediately rings again.

101
He sees it's Natalie, sends it to voicemail, and shuts off his phone. As he PASSES Sean and Coco--

JACK (CONT'D)
I guess Natalie's not coming after all.

SEAN
Oh, please, that girl? Show up at a party where she's not the center of attention?
AT THE BAR - LATER - Jack drains one drink and orders another, getting very drunk. Ali sidles up to the bar.

ALI
(TO BARTENDER)
Shot of Patron.
Jack raises his brow. Ali drinks the shot, and without looking at him--

ALI (CONT'D)
Lookin' kinda lonely.

JACK
(BOOZEY)
No. Not lonely. Liberated, yes.
Libated, absolutely. But never lonely. Cheers, baby--
He raises his glass-- she rolls her eyes, walks off-- he follows her, playfully PUSHING her from behind.

ALI
Hey-- what're we, in junior high?

JACK
You still mad at me, Iowa? C'mon.
Bring it on.
She starts to say something as-- THE SHIRELLES start to sing
"BABY IT'S YOU"-- Jack turns to the DJ, points both fingers at him and YELLS:

JACK (CONT'D)

I LOVE THIS SONG, MAN!!!

Everyone stares at the drunk guy. Ali rolls her eyes and walks off-- Jack swings her around, PULLING her close-- she just looks at him. Starts to laugh at how drunk he is-- Jack wraps her in his arms and starts to sing quietly in her ear.

JACK (CONT'D)

Many many many nights go by, I sit alone, at home and cry, over you...

ALI

Well, you're quite the crooner.
He looks her in the eye.

JACK

I'm sorry for being a class A prick.
Ali smiles, surprised at his candor. He breathes a sigh of relief.

JACK (CONT'D)

And as of about...
(bleary look at his watch,

CAN'T FOCUS)

. some time ago, I am officially a single man.

ALI

You and Natalie split up?

JACK

That we did. So. That explains what
I'm doing here all alone. What are you doing here all alone?

ALI

Do I look alone to you?
They share a look. Then he spins her around in his arms. She laughs.
AT THE BAR, tipsy Sean and Coco stand side-by-side. Coco is watching the DJ spin. The DJ glances down at them.

COCO

That DJ's hot.

SEAN

You think?

COCO

He keeps looking at me.
Coco smiles up at him, flirty. The DJ smiles back.

COCO (CONT'D)
Hmmm... I think he's cuckoo for Coco- puffs.
They look at each other, then crack up like giggling schoolgirls.

EXT. JACK'S APARTMENT - NIGHT
CLOSE ON: A KEY TRYING TO GO INTO A LOCK. Then it disappears from view. We hear it CLANK to the ground. Then giggles.

ALI (O. C.)
Whoopsie daisy --
PULL BACK to find Jack and Ali, drunk, staring at the keys on the ground.

JACK
Whoopsie daisy?

ALI
My Nanna used to say that all the time. That and upsie jumpsie.

JACK
Upsie jumpsie?
(running it together)
Upsie jumpsie, whoopsie daisy, upsie jumpsie, whoopsie daisy, upsie jumpsie --

(ABRUPTLY STOPS)
When would she say that?

ALI
When she wanted her dog to get on the bed with her. That is --

(DRUNKEN WHISPER) when she was alive.
Their eyes meet. A connection. Then, staring into her eyes:

JACK
(trying to be serious)
The dog, or Nanna?
Ali bursts out laughing. So does Jack, as he pushes the door open, and they fall into the apartment.

INT. JACK'S APARTMENT - NIGHT

Jack and Ali stumble in, Jack knocks the lamp over trying to turn on the light. It BREAKS. Ali giggles as she plops down on the couch, struggling to take off her leather boot. No luck. She holds her legs out.

ALI
Help me.
Jack gets the lamp to standing, then grabs one of Ali's boots, slides it off, dumps it. Then he tries the second -- it sticks -- he pulls harder -- the boot pops off and he careens backwards, crashing into the lamp, knocking it over again. Ali cracks up. He turns to the lamp.

JACK
(like to a dog)
Stay.
He turns back to Ali, regains composure, bows

JACK (CONT'D)
Good night.
He backs away, into the bedroom. Ali looks confused.

ALI
Oh. Okay.

(BEAT)
Good night.
Jack disappears into the bedroom and closes the door. Ali stares at it, surprised. Then resigned. Oh, well. She undoes her bra, threads it through her top and out the arms.
Then Jack's door opens. He stands in the doorway in matching
"Rudolph the Red-Nosed Reindeer" pajamas, leaning against the doorframe like Hugh Hefner in his finest silk smoking jacket.

ALI (CONT'D)
Cute jammies.

JACK
A gift from my mother. Never worn them.

ALI
Go figure.
Jack walks past Ali, toward the door.

JACK
Forgot to lock up.

(HE DOES)
Okay. Night.

ALI
Night again.
He walks back into the bedroom and once gain shuts the door.
Ali smiles to herself, plumps her pillow. The door flies open again -- Jack's there in just the pants, no top.

JACK
Water. No hangover.
He stumbles past Ali to the kitchen, drinks from the tap.
After a moment he returns to the bedroom, nodding to Ali.

JACK (CONT'D)
Night.
Ali just nods. He closes the door. Ali smiles, waiting.
After a beat, the door opens again. Jack is there, in boxers.

JACK (CONT'D)
Hungry.
He walks past her to the kitchen, opens a box of cereal, pours it into his mouth. Grabs some milk from the fridge, pours it into his mouth, too. Returns to the bedroom, crunching. He closes the door. Then -- very quickly -- he opens it again and walks out.

JACK (CONT'D)
I know I forgot something else, but
I just can't remember what...

(TO HIMSELF)
Door locked, water, food...
He wanders out into the room, past Ali, and we see from behind he is butt-ass naked. She cracks up.

JACK (CONT'D)
What's so funny?
She covers her face. He glances down.

JACK (CONT'D)
Well I never!
He strides back to the bedroom, shutting the door. After a moment, he comes back out dressed in an old, flowered bathrobe and fur-lined orange hunting cap.

JACK (CONT'D)
I remembered what I forgot to do.

ALI
What?

JACK
(SERIOUS)
Kiss you goodnight.
He crosses to her, takes her in his arms, and kisses her.
She kisses back, making up for all their lost time.
MUSIC UP: "PRISONER" a big, soulful ballad.

PAN OFF THEM TO:
INT. BURLESQUE LOUNGE - ON STAGE - NIGHT
Ali steps into frame on stage, singing:

ALI
I ' LL NEVER BE LONELY. I'LL NEVER
LOSE YOU. I 'LL NEVER BE BLUE
OR BE ALL ALONE. JUST DON'T EVER
LEAVE ME. SO MY HEART WON'T GRIEVE
ME. AND OUR GOOD LOVIN
WON'T END IN VAIN...
CARRY MUSIC AS CAMERA PANS UP OFF ALI AND DRIFTS BACK DOWN TO:
JACK'S APARTMENT - DAY
Jack and Ali in bed, in post-coital bliss.

ALI (CONT'D)
Well, it's official.

JACK
What?

ALI
You are definitely not gay.
He smiles at her, drunk with lust. CAMERA PANS UP AND OFF OF

THEM... THEN DRIFTS BACK DOWN TO:
THE CLUB - NIGHT
Ali on stage, lights blasting.

ALI (CONT'D)
OH YOUR LOVE. HAS GOT ME IN CAPTIVITY-- YEAH. YOU'LL NEVER LEAVE ME, AND I ' LL TELL YOU WHY-- YEAH. IN OTHER WORDS, IN OTHER WORDS, LISTEN, THIS IS FOREVER BABY I 'LL NEVER HAVE TO HEAR YOU SAY GOODBYE...
CAMERA PANS UP OFF ALI AND DRIFTS BACK DOWN TO:
JACK'S APARTMENT - DAY
Ali and Jack in bed, in different positions, wrapped in sheets. Jack traces the outline of her lips with his finger.

JACK
I've been wanting to do this since you first walked in the club.
She cocks an eyebrow at him.

ALI
Sure got a funny way of showing it.
He smiles at her.

JACK
I'll show you an even funnier way -- you ready?
He disappears under the sheets. She SQUEALS, starts laughing hysterically. CAMERA PANS UP AND OFF OF THEM THEN DRIFTS

BACK DOWN TO:
BURLESQUE LOUNGE - NIGHT
Ali, on stage, belting:

ALI
WE'RE JUST PRISONERS. OF OUR GOOD LOVIN. WE'RE JUST SLAVES, BOUND IN CHAINS. NO, NO, I DON ' T WANT TO EVER BE FREE, SO DON'T EVER LEAVE ME. AND OUR GOOD LOVIN, WON'T END IN VAIN...
CAMERA PANS UP OFF ALI AND DRIFTS BACK DOWN TO:
JACK'S APARTMENT - DAY
Jack in bed, sitting against the headboard, wearing only a hat. Ali's leg in the foreground, a la The Graduate, as she pulls on one fishnet stocking. Jack watches, mesmerized.

ALI (CONT'D)
So, what about Natalie... ?

JACK
Natalie who?
Ali smiles. Rolls the stocking up over her shapely thigh, then slowly takes it off. Looks at Jack. He strikes his chest, struck by cupid--

JACK (CONT'D)
Do it again.
She giggles, repeats the sexy act for him. CAMERA PANS UP AND

OFF OF THEM... THEN DRIFTS BACK DOWN TO:
THE BURLESQUE LOUNGE - NIGHT
Ali on stage, the big finish:

ALI
OH YOUR LOVE. HAS GOT ME IN
CAPTIVITY-- YEAH. YOU'LL NEVER
LEAVE ME, AND I ' LL TELL YOU WHY--
YEAH. IN OTHER WORDS, IN OTHER
WORDS, LISTEN, THIS IS FOREVER BABY
I 'LL NEVER HAVE TO HEAR YOU SAY
GOODBYE... YEAH, YEAH, YEAH, YEAH,
YEAH. WE'RE JUST PRISONERS, WE'RE
JUST PRISONERS, OF OUR GOOD LOVIN,
OF OUR GOOD LOVIN, WE 'RE JUST
SLAVE, WE'RE JUST SLAVES
BOUND IN CHAINS, BOUND IN CHAINS!
INT. JACK'S APARTMENT - BEDROOM - MORNING
Jack and Ali, twisted up in the sheets, their respective eyeliners smeared. Ali's platinum bob sticks up in all directions. Half of a fake eyelash stuck on her cheek.

EXT. JACK'S APARTMENT - THE FRONT DOOR - DAY
CLOSE ON THE LOCK as a key is inserted. The door opens.

INT. JACK'S APARTMENT - DAY
A PAIR OF WOMEN'S HEELS enter the apartment and pick their way over last night's discarded clothes and head for:

INT. JACK'S APARTMENT - BEDROOM - DAY
Where Jack and Ali are sleeping, entwined. The heels stop at the base of the bed. A beat. Then, enraged:

NATALIE
I KNEW IT!
Jack bolts up in bed. Stares.

JACK
Natalie!
Ali blinks awake. Confused.

ALI
Natalie?
Jack scrambles for something to put on.

NATALIE
YOU are a LIAR. You're a sneaky, pathetic LI-AR!

ALI
(quiet, to Jack)
What 's she doing here:

JACK
I don't know!

NATALIE
I LIVE HERE, you bleached out tramp, what the hell are YOU doing here?!!

ALI
(TO JACK)
You were engaged to this woman?

JACK
(finds his boxers)
Nat, can we talk about this in the living room --

NATALIE
I can't BELIEVE I bought your bullshit: "It's nothing, she's just this chick from work, she's nothing. "

(TO ALI)
That's what he called you.
"Nothing. She's not even pretty.
(sizing Ali up)
Well, at least you were honest about one thing--

ALI JACK
You said that? No, I didn't --

NATALIE (CONT'D) JACK
He most certainly did! Nat-- shut the fu--

ALI NATALIE
Jack?!? Don't even say his name!
As Ali grabs for a shirt--

JACK
Listen, Ali-- let me just-- would you mind --

ALI
What?!?

JACK
Giving us a little privacy?

AL I
(OFFENDED)
You want me to leave?

NATALIE
Yes you! I'm the fiancee. You're a booty call. You go.

JACK
Natalie, Jesus, STOP IT!
Ali grabs some pants from the floor, pulls them on.

ALI
Fine, I'm out of here--
(seething to Jack)
You said you split up!

NATALIE
In one phone call? Please, you don't dump a girl like me on the phone.

JACK
Both of you-- STOP IT!
As Ali quickly grabs a few things--

JACK (CONT'D)
Ali-- I'm really sorry-- I--

ALI
So am I.
She gathers up more things, really pissed--

JACK
Wait-- do you need money for a
Motel or...
Ali stifles him with an incredulous glare-- can't believe how this is going down. She looks at him, so incredibly hurt.
Grabs her suitcase and brushes past him, stuffing her belongings into it. Jack goes after her--

JACK (CONT'D)
Ali, wait a second-- don't--
(as the door SLAMS)
--go.

(BEAT)
Shit.
Jack looks at Natalie. She folds her arms.

EXT. SEAN'S APARTMENT - MORNING
Ali knocks on a door, suitcase in hand. A beat. Then a good- looking guy, who's obviously just woken up, answers with a blanket wrapped around him. He is the DJ from the wedding.

ALI
Oh. I'm sorry. I think I have the wrong apartment. I'm looking for
Sean?
(off his blank look)
Brown hair? 5'10n? Early 30's?

DJ
Oh, Sean! I thought he said John.
He's asleep. Come in.
The DJ shuffles inside. Ali follows as he leads her to the bedroom. He points to Sean in the bed.

DJ (CONT'D)
That him?

Ali nods. Sean's eyes pop open, confused to see her.

SEAN
What are you doing here?

ALI
Long story.
Sean notices the guy in the blanket.

SEAN
Ali, this is Mike.

DJ
Mark.

SEAN
Mark???

(THEN)
Oh. Anyone want coffee?

ALI
I'll make it. You two get acquainted.

INT. SEAN'S KITCHEN - DAY
Ali makes coffee, looking out the window at Hollywood. Her phone rings. She answers right away, thinking it's Jack.

ALI
HEY--
MARCUS (OVER PHONE)
Hey gorgeous.

ALI
Oh. Marcus.

MARK
(WANDERING IN)
Is the coffee ready?

MARCUS (OVER PHONE)
Who's that?

ALI
Mark. Or Mike. Jury's still out.

MARCUS (OVER PHONE)
Should I be jealous?

ALI
Only if you had your eye on Sean.

MARCUS (OVER PHONE)
You okay? You sound down.

ALI
Mmm. Maybe a little.

MARCUS (OVER PHONE)
I know just the cure.

ALI
What's that?

MARCUS (OVER PHONE)
Me. But you turned me down.
She thinks for a moment. Then:

ALI
Haven't you heard? No is the new yes.

INT. BURLESQUE LOUNGE - ON STAGE
A curtain lifts revealing a black box, FIVE GIRLS from behind seem to be floating in blackness, their curves illuminated.
They begin to move to the music (think WABASH BLUES, CRAZY HORSE SALOON) The group turns toward us--

ALI
WHAT DO YOU KNOW, HOW DO YOU DO, I LIKE THE WAY YOU LOOK AT ME WITH THOSE EYES, CONFIDENTLY WISE...
EXT. JACK'S APARTMENT - DAY
ANOTHER SLAMMING DOOR.
NATALIE'S HEELS storm away from the apartment. Carrying her bags, really PISSED, she kicks a big, fat rose blossom off a bush, and continues on.

INTERCUT WITH THE SPOTLIT STAGE
The girls continue the number. Post modern Gaultier bondage cages on top, bowler hats and black shorts. A HUMONGOUS moon hangs at the back of the theatre, the black stage awash in golden light.

ALI
PLEASURE I'M SURE, I ' VE MET YOU
BEFORE, BUT MAYBE NOT HERE, MAYBE
IT WAS, SOME OTHER TIME. THIS AIN'T
NO KIND OF PLACE FOR YOU, YOU
BETTER MOVE ALONG... I MET A GOOD
OLE' BOY WHO CAN. 00000, DON'T
FOLLOW ME DOWN. IT'S A RUSE...
EXT. SEAN'S APARTMENT - DAY - CARRY MUSIC
Marcus is waiting in his Bentley. Ali gets in. Marcus looks at her. She forces a smile. The Bentley rounds the corner as we HOLD and see JACK'S MOTORCYCLE thunder up. He gets off, runs to the building.

EXT. SEAN'S APARTMENT - STAIRWELL - DAY
Sean and Mark exchange awkward good-byes.

SEAN
Well. Bye.

MARK
You... Take care. Sean.
Mark turns, heads down the stairs as Jack rushes up, calling:

JACK
Is Ali here?

MARK
Just left.
Mark continues down. Jack whips around, looks at him, then up at Sean, who nods.

JACK
Where'd she go?

SEAN
With Marcus.

JACK
What?

SEAN
I told you, opportunity doesn't knock forever.
Jack burns, frustrated, then heads slowly down the stairs.
Sean shakes his head and turns to go back inside. Then pauses, noticing:
Mark, looking up at Sean's apartment, hesitating. Then he opens his car to get in. Sean stands there, realizing he's doing the same thing. He steps onto the stairwell. Calls out:

SEAN (CONT'D)
Hey! You!

MARK
(LOOKS UP)
It's Mark.

SEAN
Mark. You wanna have breakfast?
Off Mark's smile:

INT. MARCUS'S HOUSE - AFTERNOON
Ali follows Marcus through the kitchen, to the fridge.

MARCUS
My mother always said there's only one thing to do when you're feeling blue...
He opens the fridge and pulls out a bottle of CHAMPAGNE.

ALI
She was a poet.

MARCUS
And a drunk.
Ali smiles. Marcus pops the cork, fills two glasses, hands her one. Clinks.

MARCUS (CONT'D)
To your new place.

ALI
What new place?

INT. MARCUS'S HOUSE - GUEST HOUSE - DAY
A lavish, 1000-square-foot guest house. Marcus ushers Ali in.

MARCUS

All yours.
(off her look)
Unpack. Move in.

ALI
Marcus, I can't just--

MARCUS
Sure you can.
Marcus plops her suitcase on the bed.

MARCUS (CONT'D)
Unpack. You're home.

ALI
It's not even on the bus route.

MARCUS
Okay, that is the first and last time the term "bus route" will be spoken in this house.
(motions out window)
Four cars. Which do you want?

EXT. MARCUS'S GAZEBO - SUNSET
Ali lies on a chaise overlooking the panoramic view of L. A. against a fiery red sky. Marcus comes out of the house, with a bottle of wine. Crosses and sits next to her on the chaise.
Marcus refills their wine glasses. An empty bottle already there. She sips as she leans back and relaxes.

MARCUS
Better?

ALI
(SMILES)
Better.
She looks out at a giant billboard at eye level.

MARCUS
You're gonna be on one of those someday.

ALI
Yeah, right.

MARCUS
Sooner than you think, too. Harold
Saint called me today. You made quite an impression on him.

ALI
Really? What'd he say?

MARCUS
He wants to make a demo with you.

ALI
Are you serious? When??

MARCUS
He found a little studio time on
Tuesday.

ALI
This Tuesday?

MARCUS
Too soon?

ALI
No! Oh my god, no, that's amazing.
You're amazing.

MARCUS
I like making you happy. Your whole face lights up.
Their eyes meet. He pushes some hair out of her face.

ALI
I think you're way too nice to me.

MARCUS
And that's a problem because...

ALI
I've had a lot to drink. And my judgment is off.
He touches her face, their chemistry palpable.

MARCUS
Hey, I'm a gentleman. Which means

I'd never kiss a lady when she's... vulnerable.
She looks at him.

ALI
Liar.
She leans in and impulsively pulls him into a kiss.

INT. JACK'S APARTMENT - DAY
Jack, alone now, collects the clothes Ali left behind. He reaches under the couch and sees the PHOTO of Ali and her mother. He picks it up, smooths out the cracks. Traces 7- year-old Ali's face with his fingertips.

INT. MARCUS'S HOUSE - GUEST HOUSE - DAY
Ali lies in a tangle of 1000-thread-count sheets. Her eyes blink open. She sits up alone, getting her bearings.

ALI
Where am I?
She sees a Warhol-esque PRINT OF MARCUS on the wall. She raises her brows then sees her disheveled reflection in a huge mirror: smeared mascara, hair askew.

ALI (CONT'D)
Who am I?
She sees her and Marcus's clothes in a trail on the floor and bites her lip, remembering last night.

INT. MARCUS'S LIVING ROOM - MORNING
Ali, freshly showered, enters, a stranger in a strange land.
STAFF is milling around. She HEARS a SPLASH. Looks out the glass windows, sees Marcus swimming laps. The HOUSEKEEPER passes her, nods "morning". Ali smiles.
Then she notices a long table full of miniature MODELS of
BUILDINGS. She takes them in, pausing at a tall, sleek MODEL of a glass HIGH-RISE, towering over the other models.
She runs her finger lightly over it, intrigued. Then she sees the address marker: 7800 Sunset Blvd.
Ali stares, stunned. Marcus enters, toweling himself dry.

MARCUS
Morning.
He comes up behind her, nuzzles her neck.

ALI
What is this?

MARCUS
Now it's a model. But when it grows up, it'll be a mixed-use space: retail and residential.

ALI
This is the address of the
Burlesque Lounge.
Marcus shrugs, dries his hair.

MARCUS
Best view on the Sunset Strip, with no windows. When I'm done with it, it'll have a thousand.

ALI
You can't tear down the club.

MARCUS
Actually, I can.

ALI
But what about the history? That place is a landmark.

MARCUS
Not according to the city.

ALI
Does Tess know about this?

MARCUS
What Tess knows and doesn't know isn't a big concern of mine.

ALI
What makes you think she would ever sell the Lounge?

MARCUS
She has no choice. She's going under.

ALI
But that club is her life!

MARCUS
Oh, come on, you get this. It's business. It's not personal.

ALI
Not personal? It's pretty god damn personal for Tess! And Coco and Sean and Alexis. And what about Jesse? And Dave the lighting guy?

MARCUS
ALI --
ALI
And what about me? It's pretty God damn personal to me.
She turns to leave.

MARCUS
Where are you going?

ALI
To the club. Where I work.
She marches out of the room, resolute--

MARCUS
Ali-- wait!!!
At the door she turns back and looks at him. As he starts to speak, she SLAMS the door shut as we HEAR "THAT'S LIFE".

INT. BURLESQUE LOUNGE - ON STAGE - LATE AFTERNOON
Eva Destruction does a sexy contortionist number on stage as the Tattooed Bumper Band plays "THAT'S LIFE" with her.
CLOSE ON - a LINE OF SHOT GLASSES. Tequila is poured. The Bartenders behind the bar, Jack sits on a stool on the other side, his bags packed beside him. They all pick up their shot glasses, toast and drink as they begin to sing "THAT'S LIFE" in a rousing, fun, guys number.

THE BARTENDERS AND JACK
THAT ' S LIFE, THAT ' S WHAT ALL THE
PEOPLE SAY.
YOU'RE RIDING HIGH IN APRIL,
SHOT DOWN IN MAY
BUT I KNOW I'M GONNA CHANGE THAT TUNE,
WHEN I'M BACK ON TOP, BACK ON TOP IN JUNE.
EXT. PARKING LOT - AFTERNOON - CARRY MUSIC
Tess pulls into the lot-- gets out of her car dressed to the nines in a tailored business suit, hair up, professional. She HEADS into the club--

INT. BURLESQUE LOUNGE - SAME

As Eva performs and the Bartenders and Jack sing, SEAN looks up at Dave, and MOTIONS for the SPOTLIGHT on Jack. Dave nods, and SWINGS the SPOTLIGHT hitting JACK. The Bartenders push
Jack up onto the bar as he TAKES THE LEAD--

JACK
. I SAID THAT'S LIFE, AND AS FUNNY
AS IT MAY SEEM
SOME PEOPLE GET THEIR KICKS,
STOMPIN' ON A DREAM
BUT I DON'T LET IT, LET IT GET ME DOWN,
'CAUSE THIS FINE OL' WORLD IT KEEPS
SPINNING AROUND...
I'VE BEEN A PUPPET, A PAUPER, A
PIRATE, A POET, A PAWN AND A KING.
I'VE BEEN UP AND DOWN AND OVER AND
OUT AND I KNOW ONE THING:
EACH TIME I FIND MYSELF, FLAT ON MY
FACE, I PICK MYSELF UP AND GET BACK
IN THE RACE...

The whole club is with him now, as Jack channels Sinatra, standing on the bar-- the Bartenders sing back-up.

JACK (CONT'D)
THAT'S LIFE. THAT'S LIFE AND I
CAN'T DENY IT. MANY TIMES I THOUGHT
OF CUTTING OUT, BUT MY HEART WON'T
BUY IT. BUT IF THERE ' S NOTHING
SHAKIN' COME THIS HERE JULY...
I'M GONNA ROLL MYSELF UP IN A BIG
BALL AND DIE. MY, MY.

Applause, hoots and hollers. Jack high-fives and fist pumps his buddies, hugs Sean, grabs his bag and suitcase and EXITS out the back as...
Tess ENTERS. SEES Sean is at the bar. He looks up--

SEAN
How'd it go?
(sees her face)
Oh, shit.
She grabs a bottle of Tequila and a glass, turns to walk off.

SEAN (CONT'D)

What are you gonna do?

TESS
Right now? Get really drunk.
THE FRONT DOORS OPEN, and Ali ENTERS, spots Tess, rushes over to her.

ALI
Tess! I have to talk to you!
Tess keeps walking.

ALI (CONT'D)
Marcus Gerber is trying to buy the lounge, and he's gonna tear it down and build a twenty-story skyscraper!
Tess stops. Slowly turns and stares at Ali, who's suddenly embarrassed to admit...

ALI (CONT'D)
I just saw the plans.
Tess looks at Ali. Stunned. Ali stands there, breathless, waiting for her reaction. But Tess just turns, continues up to her office, and shuts the door. Ali turns to Sean-- then starts after her--

ALI (CONT'D)
She has to do something! She can't just let him --

SEAN
(STOPPING HER)
Let it go, girl. She just got turned down for another loan. It's either foreclose, or sell to Marcus.

ALI
So that's it? It's over?

SEAN
The circle of life, baby. All good things must come to an end.

ALI
But she can't just give up!

SEAN
She's not giving up. She's going down with her ship. With dignity.
Ali sits on a barstool, in disbelief.

SEAN (CONT'D)

I've got something for you.
He pulls out the photo of Ali with her mother. It's in a new frame.

ALI
Where'd you get this?

SEAN
Jack. He dropped it off on his way to the airport.

ALI
Where's he going?

SEAN
New York on the red-eye.

ALI
To be with Natalie?

SEAN
Pedal faster, baby, he and Natalie are over. You're the one he's been looking high and low for.

ALI
(TOUCHED)
Really... ?

(THEN:)
Then why's he going to New York?

SEAN
(duh!)
Get your ass over to LAX and ask him yourself!
Ali nods, jumps up from her stool, and races for the door, then stops, realizing:

ALI
I don't have a --
Sean tosses her his CAR KEYS.

SEAN
American to JFK. Go!
Ali catches the keys and TAKES OFF.
- EXT. PARKING LOT - NIGHT - Ali (in a Prius) peels out of the lot, weaving through traffic as she lifts her cell.

- INT. AIRPORT - NIGHT - CLOSE SHOT: a CELL PHONE in a plastic bowl moves through a security X-ray machine.

JACK'S VOICE
This is Jack. Leave me a message.
FIND Jack on the other side, as his belongings come down the conveyor belt. He grabs them, turns off his cell.
- EXT. STREET - NIGHT - ALI skids through a light, veers past cars.
- INT. CONCOURSE - NIGHT Jack reaches gate 43, sees a long line. Gets in back.
- INT. AIRPORT TERMINAL - NIGHT - Ali bolts through the front door, frantically checks the DEPARTURES MONITOR.
Finds: NEW YORK JFK, GATE 43: NOW BOARDING.
- INT. TERMINAL - NIGHT - Ali races up the escalator, approaching SECURITY.

SECURITY GUY
Boarding pass?

AL I
I have to talk to someone, he's --

SECURITY GUY
No one's allowed past this point without a boarding pass.

ALI
But I have to speak to him!

SECURITY GUY
I'm sorry, miss.

ALI
I HAVE TO GET TO GATE 43!
SECURITY GUY
There's Gate 43, right over there.
He points. It's the first gate beyond Security. Ali sees
Jack, in line, about to board the plane. He's wearing his iPod headset, deaf to the world.

ALI
JACK! JACK! JACK!
ALL HEADS TURN to look at her, except Jack, who can't hear.
A PLUMP WOMAN in front of him looks at Ali. Ali points to
Jack. The woman taps Jack and points. He looks to see:
ALI, on the other side of Security. Jack takes his earphones off and smiles. He crosses over to her, carrying his bag.

They are separated by several feet of security ropes.

JACK
What are you doing here?

ALI
Sean told me you're going to New
York. Please don't go!

JACK
I have to. I got an offer from that band -- the Punk Fusion group. They want me to tour with them.

ALI
Really?

JACK
They finally had it with the flaky keyboardist. I'll be back in five weeks. Will you be here?

ALI
Yes! Yes. Absolutely.

JACK
What about Marcus?

ALI
. Marcus who?
They share a smile, separated by the ropes.

JACK
I'm trying to figure out if I should kiss you now, or make you wait five weeks.

ALI
Five weeks?! That's forever!
ANGLE ON: A MALE AND FEMALE SECURITY GUARD, listening to the whole exchange.

ATTENDANT (ON P. A.)
FINAL BOARDING FOR FLIGHT 673 TO
NEW YORK, JFK AT GATE 43
JACK
I gotta go, that's me.

He picks up his bags. It's killing Ali.

JACK (CONT'D)
I'll call you when I get there.
Take care of Miles Davis.
(off Ali's confusion)
Our cat. I named him.
They smile again. Neither wanting this moment to end. She waves. He nods. Then he turns and walks off to board. Ali watches him go.
ON JACK, walking back to the gate-then -- he stops. Turns back to see Ali, but she's gone.

FEMALE SECURITY GUARD
Boy, you get out there and kiss that girl! Now!
Jack looks at her, then quickly turns to walk past the Male Security Guard.

MALE SECURITY GUARD
Go ahead-- but you're gonna have to come back through Security again.

JACK
But then I'll miss my flight!

FEMALE SECURITY GUARD
Martin! Don't you dare keep that boy from kissing his girl!
Martin looks at Jack. Then:

MALE SECURITY GUARD
Ah, hell. Go ahead. Bag stays here.
Jack drops his bag, takes a running JUMP over the ROPES and RUNS through the crowded concourse -- startling everyone.
ON ALI, as she walks through the concourse, reliving her last sight of Jack. As she's about to get on the escalator:

JACK
ALI!
She turns. Jack is there. In one fantastically romantic move, he pulls her into his arms, kisses her deeply -- an epic kiss that makes passersby stop and stare.

ATTENDANT (ON P. A.)
FINAL BOARDING CALL FOR FLIGHT 673
TO NEW YORK JFK AT GATE
Jack looks at Ali.

ALI
Well, go get 'em, Jack.
He smiles, then disappears into the crowd. Ali stands there, watching him, gobsmacked by the kiss.

EXT. BURLESQUE LOUNGE - LATE NIGHT
Sean's car whips into the parking lot. Ali jumps out and heads for the front entrance. The CONSTRUCTION WORKERS from the towering building across the street HOOT and CAT-CALL at her. She waves to them and nods: that's right, boys.

INT. BURLESQUE LOUNGE - NIGHT
Ali enters just as Tess, in a spotlight on stage, turns toward the audience. She looks fabulous. Only someone who knows her really well could tell she's dying inside.

TESS
Smoother than honey and twice as sweet. Each girl lovelier then the next. Gentlemen, hold onto your hats. Ladies, hold on to your gentlemen. We may not have windows... but we DO have...
(motions to the girls)
. the best view on the Sunset
Strip.
The audience hoots as the Burlesque Girls ENTER the stage dancing. (SONG TBD)
ON ALI-- a lightbulb going on! As Tess exits the stage, Ali pushes through the crowd and races backstage.

INT. BURLESQUE LOUNGE - BACKSTAGE - NIGHT
Tess is arriving in her office, defeated, as Ali bursts in behind her.

ALI
Tess!

TESS
You could knock-- this is still my office--at least for another 48

HOURS--
ALI
But this is really, really --
Tess holds up a hand.

TESS
Not. Now.

ALI
BUT--
TESS
I said -- NOT --

ALI
Yes now! God damn, you are one stubborn mule of a woman. Anyone else in their right mind would have figured out by now, when I have something to tell you, you listen!
I told you I could dance, did you listen? No. Big mistake. I told you I could sing, did you listen?
No. Big. mistake. This time you are going to hear what I have to say if
I have to tie you up with your corset strings and scream it in your God damn ear.
For the first time someone silences Tess. Ali takes a breath.

ALI (CONT'D)
Have you ever heard of air rights?

EXT. LOFT BUILDING HALLWAY - DAY
TWO SETS OF FIERCE HEELS and LEGS stride in unison down a sidewalk. PAN UP as Tess and Ali enter:

INT. LOFT BUILDING - SALES OFFICE - DAY
A smartly-dressed BUSINESSMAN sits at his mahogany desk deep in a phone conversation as WHAM! The door to his office flies open and Ali and Tess stride in, an overwrought assistant on their heels.

BUSINESSMAN
(INTO PHONE)
Jim -- Jim -- hang on, I'm gonna have to call you back -- Jim!
Damnit, Nancy, get him back.
Assistant scurries out. Businessman turns to Tess.

BUSINESSMAN (CONT'D)
Back with more noise complaints?

TESS
You offered to buy my club a few years back. I said no.

BUSINESSMAN
And now you've changed your mind.

TESS
Not exactly.

Tess smiles at him. Looks at Ali, who's not smiling. She elbows her. Ali starts smiling. Tess walks up to the desk and sits herself down. Ali does the same.

BUSINESSMAN
I'm confused.

TESS
Go with me, there's a good ending,
I promise. How much will these condos you're building sell for?

BUSINESSMAN
They start at one million and go up, depending on the view.

TESS
What if I told you a twenty-story high-rise was going up where my club is?

(TO ALI)
Would twenty stories block his view?

ALI
Ten stories would. Twenty would decimate them. Leaving behind a lot of angry homeowners staring across the street at fluorescent light bulbs and dirty windows.

TESS
So. Mr. ?

BUSINESSMAN
Anderson.

TESS
Mr. Anderson. Your pretty million- dollar ocean views are going away because I'm selling my building to a developer tomorrow who'll have his twenty stories all framed up by the time you start selling --

ALI
Trying to sell--

TESS
Trying to sell these condos.

(BEAT)
Or. I can put you in a position where your buyers could be guaranteed their million-dollar views forever.

BUSINESSMAN
I'm listening.

TESS
As am I. As long as you're telling me you'll have a check to me by 5:00 today.

INT. BURLESQUE LOUNGE - EVENING
The BUMPER BAND PLAYS. Vince sits with his POSSE. His cocktail waitress/girlfriend approaches with an empty tray.
She whispers to him:

COCKTAIL WAITRESS
Sorry, baby, they cut you off at the bar. Said you have to pay cash.

VINCE
What? I co-own this goddamn place--
Tess comes up behind him.

TESS
Not anymore you don't. I'm buying you out.

VINCE
You can't do that.

TESS
Actually, according to page 4 of our contract, I can.

VINCE
(SCOFFING)
In the next 48 hours?

TESS
Why postpone joy?
She hands him a CASHIER'S CHECK. Vince stares at it.

VINCE
What the hell is this?

TESS
I realize it's been a while since you've seen one, but it's called a check.
He stares at it, stunned. Then at her.

VINCE
Where'd you get this?

TESS
Not your business anymore. And neither is the lounge.

(POINTS)
I'm sure you know where the door is. It used to be half yours.
(re. the waitress)
And take HER with you.
Tess turns and goes over to the bar, where Ali spins around on her barstool, having heard the whole thing.

ALI
How'd that feel?

TESS
Not half bad.
Tess parks it next to her. Looks at Ali. Smiles, then breaks into a giggle. Ali smiles. Tess laughs even harder, tears in her eyes now. They are just two girls laughing hysterically at the bar, Tess keeps trying to say something, but can't get it out, until she looks Ali square in the eye...

TESS (CONT'D)
It felt pretty God damn awesome!
And they crack up again. Then...

ALI
And to think, you didn't even want me around.

TESS
Oh, Jesus, here it comes.

ALI
. What was it you said to me that first night? "Twenty bucks at the door will make all your dreams come true. " That was sweet of you.

TESS
Are you finished?

ALI
(loving needling her)

Kinda ironic, when you think about it. I started off begging you to make my dreams come true, and here we are --

TESS
All right already! You want me to say it, I'll say it.
She looks at her.

TESS (CONT'D)
This place is the love of my life.
The only dream I've ever had. I don't know what I would have done if I had lost it.

(HEARTFELT NOW)
Thank you.
A moment between them... as Tess SPOTS NIKKI ENTER the club carrying her dance bag--a little fresher than we've seen her before, and sober. Nikki looks over at Tess... then approaches. Ali turns away on her bar stool, respectfully.

NIKKI
(SHEEPISH)
I crossed the line.
Tess crosses her arms, and with a smirk on her face--

TESS
Again.

NIKKI
Again, and I wanna come home--

TESS
AGAIN--
NIKKI
Yes, again! Did you fill my spot or what... ?

TESS
What do you think?
Tess and Nikki share a look.

TESS (CONT'D)
Curtain's up in Shake a leg.
Nikki smiles, hikes her dance bag over her shoulder and heads

BACKSTAGE--
Ali looks at Tess quizzically--

ALI
Just like that?

TESS
If I had a dollar for every time she's quit...

ALI
Really?

TESS
We all fight. Bitch. Love and hate.
And then make up. Just like sisters.

ALI
I never had a sister.

TESS
Me neither. THANK GOD.

(THEN)
(MORE)
TESS (CONT'D)
Now get your cute little ass and big ole' voice up on stage, cause this is Burlesque, baby girl, where the women are always on top, and the men like it that way. Like I've always said --

ALI/TESS
You can't keep a good girl down.

BACKSTAGE DRESSING ROOM
Ali walks into the dressing room. Sits down in front of her mirror. Across the room, Nikki is sitting at hers. Ali looks at Nikki in the reflection of her mirror. Their eyes meet. Then Nikki nods. And Ali nods back. For the first time, a mutual respect.
All the other girls begin to pour into the dressing room.
Chatting, gossiping, changing their clothes. The legs, boobs, fishnets, etc. Things back the way there were, and the way they'll always be.
ON ALI. She looks at herself in the mirror. Picks up the make- up brush Tess gave her. Dips it in water. Then applies a line on her eye expertly. She smiles to herself. MUSIC UP: A heavy bass drumlin beat which takes us to...

INT. BURLESQUE LOUNGE - NIGHT - CARRY MUSIC
A SPOTLIGHT. MOVING down the smoke-filled shaft of light as--

A FIGURE RISES into view at the back of the stage. Over the contemporary BEAT, we HEAR a beautiful classic opera

(Carmen?) REVEAL... it's NIKKI! She sings a line or two in an amazing operatic voice that totally blows us away. Then ... a

DANCE BEAT KICKS IN as COCO comes into view, and sings another line. Then Jessie. Then Scarlett. And FINALLY...

Ali RISES into view, wearing a diamond studded Gaultier-type harness top and sequined hot-pants. This song (to be written) is a contemporary dance song about BURLESQUE with a vintage feel to it. Nikki and the Burlesque Girls, in similar costumes, back Ali as she SINGS her big finale. CAMERA MOVES through the packed house as we SEE Georgia, Sean, Mark (the

DJ) and Tess, who double-takes at MR. ANDERSON (the

Businessman) who sees her and smiles.

ON STAGE, ALI and the entire company explode in a surreal whirl of dancing. Turning. Kicking. Arched backs. Legs overhead. Rhinestones. Garters. Fishnets. The entire company, band and bartenders join in an all out BOLLYWOOD FINALE.

CAMERA MOVES INTO THE CLUB as music CROSSFADES with the

SOUNDS of people TALKING. Glasses CLINKING. All the background sounds of a busy nightclub. A LOUD DRUM ROLL takes us to...

A LOW CAMERA moving across a black stage as we MOVE IN ON the footlights which become a MILLION BRILLIANT LIGHTS blasting into camera, blinding us until they form letters reading:

BURLESQUE

Made in the USA
Las Vegas, NV
06 May 2026